Creating & Recognizing
Quality Rubrics

Creating & Recognizing Quality Rubrics

Judith A. Arter and Jan Chappuis

PEARSON
Merrill
Prentice Hall

Upper Saddle River, New Jersey
Columbus, Ohio

Cover design: Machele Brass, Brass Design
Book design and typesetting: Heidi Bay, Grey Sky Design
Editing: Robert L. Marcum, editorbob.com
Project coordination: Barbara Fankhauser

To obtain permission to use ETS copyrighted material contact the
Permissions Administrator by email at permissions@ets.org or by mail at:

Educational Testing Service
Office of the General Counsel
ATTN: Permissions Administrator
Rosedale Road, MS 04-C
Princeton, NJ 08541

This special edition is published by Merrill Prentice Hall, by
arrangement with Educational Testing Service.

Vice President and Executive Publisher: Jeffery W. Johnston
Publisher: Kevin M. Davis
Director of Marketing: David Gesell
Marketing Manager: Autumn Purdy
Marketing Coordinator: Brian Mounts

This book was printed and bound by Edwards Brothers. The cover
was printed by Phoenix Color Corp.

**Published 2007 by Pearson Education, Inc., Upper Saddle
River, New Jersey 07458.**
Pearson Prentice Hall. All rights reserved. Printed in the United States
of America.

10 9 8 7 6 5 4 3 2 1
ISBN-13:   978-0-13-513420-7
ISBN-10:   0-13-513420-X

Preface

Rubrics are no longer a new idea. Their capacity to assist students in acquiring complex reasoning proficiencies and skills has been repeatedly studied and well documented through research. However, rubrics can only have this effect if you construct them well and use them judiciously, and it is our intent with this book to help you do just that. We draw from over 20 years of direct experience with developing rubrics and performance tasks, devising interesting ways to use rubrics as teaching tools in the classroom, employing rubrics to score thousands of pieces of student work for classroom and large-scale assessments, and working with teachers to make their rubrics more instructionally powerful. We have written with the practicing teacher as our primary audience, but preservice teachers will also find applicable content.

The world of performance assessment and rubrics has changed significantly in a short time. Research on the effects of using rubrics instructionally in the classroom has led to increased emphasis on a variety of formative assessment practices. More teachers are actively using performance assessments in the classroom in an effort to evaluate important content standards. And, most significantly, especially for students, the education community is beginning to balance its reliance on external assessment systems with an understanding of classroom assessment's instructional power.

These developments have led to the flowering of a plethora of rubrics; the world is awash with rubrics. When writing this book, we set out to make easier the task of sifting through all that is available to find those that will work best for you and for your students. We have explained how to create your own rubric should you come up empty handed. In addition, we have included chapters on related topics necessary to maximizing student success: recognizing quality performance tasks, using rubrics instructionally, and communicating with parents about rubrics.

Whatever your role in education, we hope that reading our book saves you time in the long run and enhances the competence of both you and your students.

Acknowledgments

We are indebted to many individuals who have contributed directly or indirectly to the creation of this book. They have taught us, influenced our thinking, and helped us craft the finished product. Their contributions deserve acknowledgement and our gratitude.

We thank those with whom we have discussed ideas and shared insights and materials over the years. Foremost among these have been Vicki Spandel and Ruth Culham, the superstars of the Six Plus One Traits of Writing, who started us down the path of using rubrics as tools for learning 25 years ago, and Rick Stiggins, a proponent of performance assessment and its use in the classroom as early as 1984. Others who have helped shape our thinking are Donna Snodgrass, assessment director of the Cleveland Metropolitan School District, Kathy Busick, and Jay McTighe. Added to these are the many teachers who have both shared their rubrics and ideas with us and kept us in touch with the realities of day-to-day life with students.

Guardian of grammar, our editor Robert L. Marcum, and maven of manuscripts, our text designer Heidi Bay, enhanced the expression of our thoughts at every step. Their talents helped translate this book from a collection of ideas to a polished product.

Finally, we thank the people we work with daily: Barbara Fankhauser, who assisted with the production process; Sharon Lippert and Mindy Dotson, who painstakingly proofed manuscript after manuscript; Laura Camacho, who helped us with whatever we asked; and Steve Chappuis and Rick Stiggins, who contributed many insightful comments and suggestions. We are grateful for their support and sustained good nature toward us.

Table of Contents

chapter
$$\left[\ 1\ \right]$$

Defining *Rubric*

Ultimately, we want students to grow to be independent.
For them to do that, they have to have a sense of what the
criteria [are] that make them successful. For a long time, the
criteria [have] been a mystery to students.

—R. J. Tierney, M. Carter, & L. Desai
Portfolio Assessment in the Reading–Writing Classroom,
Norwood, MA: Christopher-Gordon, 1991, p. 4

1

What do you think of when you hear the words *rubric, scoring guide,* or *criteria*? Do you think of standards? Indicators of quality? What counts? What's important? These terms are used in many ways, often interchangeably; there is no one right usage. We use the following definitions in this book:

A *rubric* defines the features of work that constitute quality. It is the mechanism for judging the quality of student work.

A *scoring guide* is the same thing as a *rubric*. We'll use these two terms interchangeably.

Criteria (also called *traits*) are the major dimensions of work that are important.

Whatever you call them, rubrics are not ends in themselves. They are tools to help teachers teach and students learn.

Contexts for Rubrics

Helping Teachers

Rubrics are a good way to help teachers define complex learning targets and ensure that judgments about student work are consistent over time, between assignments, and with colleagues.

What are our criteria for evaluating a restaurant? For Olympic diving? For giving an oral presentation? These criteria tend to roll easily off our tongues. In a restaurant we value good food, good service, a nice ambience, reasonable prices, cleanliness, and so on. In Olympic diving the criteria relate to the form of the diver and her entry into the water. A good oral presentation involves interesting content presented in a manner that engages the audience.

But, what are our criteria for critical thinking? Being a lifelong learner? Communicating in mathematics? These are a little harder. And yet, as teachers, we are asked to develop these qualities in our students. How can we do that if it is a little fuzzy in our heads what it looks like when students are hitting the target? Even trickier: What does it look like when students are at a beginning or intermediate level of achievement on the reasoning proficiencies, performance skills, and product development we want?

If you are thinking, "Rubrics, what a wonderful way to be consistent in marking, keeping track of student progress over time, and planning instruction," then you are thinking of rubrics as a tool to help teachers.

Helping Students

In addition to helping teachers, good rubrics help students.

Do students always know what is expected of them? Do students understand what it looks like to write well, give a good oral presentation, work well in a group, analyze information, or think critically? Rubrics help students by orienting them to what it is they are expected to accomplish, efficiently leading them along the continuum from beginner to expert, and helping them be able to explain why products and performances they create are good or not. As Rick Stiggins often says, "Students can hit any target that is sufficiently clear and that holds still for them."

If you are thinking, "Rubrics, what a wonderful way to let students know what it looks like when work is good, and get students involved in their own learning to boost achievement," then you are thinking about rubrics as a way to help students.

Rubrics as Part of Assessment *of* and *for* Learning

Both of these perspectives—helping teachers and helping students—are important. There is a body of research on the impact on student learning of using rubrics in the ways stated previously. This impact ranges from minimal to large depending on the quality of the rubrics and the depth of use with students. We have yet to see a study that shows that using high-quality rubrics with students has a negative effect on student learning. A partial list of impact studies is provided in the Bibliography at the end of the book. Several of these references are summaries of many studies over time.

The conclusion? Rubrics improve achievement if designed and used well. This book is about designing and using rubrics effectively, to maximize their impact on student learning.

Using rubrics is not the whole story of how classroom assessment can improve student learning, however. It is one in an ever-increasing arsenal of strategies being called *assessment* for *learning*. This term, first used by the Assessment Reform Group in the United Kingdom in 2001, is now in use internationally.

Assessment for *learning* seeks to use the assessment process and products to improve student learning. We contrast it with assessment of *learning*, which seeks to report the status of a given student at a point in time. One is not better than the other; they serve different purposes. Assessment *of* learning seeks to determine status; assessment *for* learning seeks to improve the achievement being measured. Rubrics can be used for either purpose. Use of rubrics to grade is assessment *of* learning. Teacher use of rubrics to help students understand the achievement targets they are to hit, plan instruction, and give descriptive feedback to students is assessment *for* learning, as is student use of rubrics to clarify what quality work looks like, self-assess, set goals for next steps in instruction, and communicate with others about their progress in learning.

In addition to the research that focuses on rubrics, a substantial research base demonstrates that if assessment *for* learning strategies are used in the classroom, student achievement can improve dramatically. A sampling of studies on assessment *for* learning is included in the Bibliography at the end of the book. Gains reported typically fall between .5 and 1.0 standard deviation. Translated into the school context, this represents an additional gain of 30 to 40 percentile points on a standardized test. This size gain would have moved the United States from 21st place to the top 5 on the Third International Mathematics and Science Study. That's a lot of growth. We describe how to use rubrics as assessment *for* learning in Chapter 6.

Types of Assessments Requiring Rubrics and Scoring Guides

Any assessment that asks students to construct a response longer than a few words rather than selecting an answer from a list requires a rubric or scoring guide. Assessment methods that ask students to select an answer from a list include our old friends multiple choice, matching, and true-false. These can be evaluated for correctness with a scoring key.

When students compose a response that requires a judgment of the degree of quality, it helps to have some guidelines for how to make those judgments consistently. What's going to count? How much is it going to count? What are you looking for in the response? Guidelines for making judgments—rubrics—are helpful for the following types of assessments:

- *Performance assessment*—Assessment based on observation and judgment. You watch students do something (a performance), or create something (a product) and you judge its quality.

- *Extended written response*—Students write out their response to questions such as why they solved a problem as they did, how something works, why something happened (or did not happen) as it did, how things are alike and different, and so on.

- *Extended oral response*—Students answer questions orally such as why they solved a problem as they did, how something works, why something happened (or did not happen) as it did, how things are alike and different, and so on.

Types of Rubrics

Rubrics come in several different forms, all of which you may have encountered in published materials, your state or provincial assessments, or your own practice. The varieties are all viable options depending on what you are trying to assess and the purpose for giving the assessment. It is common practice to distinguish between *analytic* and *holistic* rubrics as well as between *task-specific* and *general* rubrics (see, e.g., Danielson, 1997; Herman, Baker, & Linn, 2004; McTighe & Wiggins, 1999; Mertler, 2001; Moskal, 2000; National Council of Teachers of Mathematics, 2003; Perlman, 2004).

Comparing Holistic and Analytic Rubrics

Consider a car engine. How well the engine runs overall can be judged. Such a judgment is *holistic*—the engine is examined as a whole. But, the engine consists of parts that work together to make the whole engine run well or poorly; they can be examined separately for quality. In this case you're analyzing the engine by examining its component parts—such judgments are *analytic*.

So it is with complex student products or performances. In student work, we usually have a list of attributes—called *criteria* or *traits*—that work together to create a product or performance of various levels of quality, just as the parts of an engine work together to make it run well or poorly. If we consider the parts all together to come up with a single judgment of how good the product or performance is overall, rating is *holistic*—we've considered the product or performance as a whole. On the other hand, we engage in *analytical* rating when we analyze the product or performance by looking at each of its relevant component parts.

If any part of the engine is a little off, it doesn't run as well, just as if any trait is off, the whole products or performance doesn't work as well.

An example of each type of rubric is shown in Figure 1.1 and Table 1.1.

Figure 1.1 Example of an Analytic Rubric for "Evaluating the Whole Portfolio"

This rubric has five criteria: *Change Over Time, Diversity, Evidence of Thinking, Self-Reflection*, and *Structure and Organization*. Each criterion has three levels defined. We have reproduced two of these criteria here. The entire rubric can be found in Appendix C and on the accompanying CD.

Diversity

Strong—The portfolio clearly demonstrates that the student has tried a variety of tasks/projects/assignments/challenges. There is great variety in the kinds of work presented or the outcomes/skills demonstrated. For instance, a math portfolio might include some problem analysis, samples of graphing skill, a problem-solving task that shows more than one solution, good use of math terminology, and a project showing application of math skills.

Developing—The portfolio reflects some diversity. Tasks are not all parallel and do not all demonstrate identical outcomes. For instance, a math portfolio might include open-ended problem solving with analysis of how the student did the task together with samples showing correct application of math procedures, concepts, or symbols.

Not Yet—The portfolio reflects minimal diversity. All tasks represented are more or less alike and demonstrate the same outcomes/skills.

Self-Reflection

Strong—Several (or more) examples of self-reflection show thoughtful consideration of personal strengths and needs based on in-depth understanding of criteria. Reflections may also include a statement of personal goals; responses to learning, to a unit of study, or to an assignment; a summary of growth over time; or other insight regarding the personal, individual story this student's portfolio tells.

Developing—Self-reflections included within the portfolio provide at least a superficial analysis of strengths and needs, which may or may not be tied to specific criteria for judging performance or growth. The student may include comments on what he/she likes or dislikes about a content area or unit of study, or about what he/she finds difficult or challenging; but the reflections may not include insights regarding growth, needs, goals, or changes in performance or learning styles over time.

Figure 1.1 (Continued)

> **Not Yet**—Either no self-reflection is included within the portfolio, or the self-reflection is rudimentary: e.g., "I put this in because I like it"; "I included this in my portfolio because it took me a long time to do it"; or "This is in my portfolio because we were asked to put it in."

Source: From Northwest Regional Educational Laboratory, 1999. Used with permission.

Table 1.1 Example of a Holistic Rubric for a Math Portfolio

Level 4: Excellent	The portfolio shows mathematics work consisting of a variety of topics and activities. The student selects examples of work that illustrates correct mathematics and thinking. The portfolio shows evidence that the student can describe why the pieces of work were selected.
Level 3: Awesome	The portfolio shows mathematics work consisting of a variety of topics and activities. The student selects work that illustrates mostly correct mathematics and thinking. The portfolio shows evidence that the student can often describe why the pieces of work were selected.
Level 2: Good	The portfolio shows mathematics work with limited topics and activities. The student selects examples of work that illustrate some errors in mathematics and thinking. The portfolio shows some evidence that the student periodically describes why the pieces of work were selected.
Level 1: OK	The portfolio shows a collection of student work with many errors. The student offers little explanation of why the pieces of work were chosen.

Source: From *Mathematics Assessment: A Practical Handbook for Grades K–12* (p. 97), by National Council of Teachers of Mathematics, 2003, Reston, VA: Author. Reprinted with permission.

Activity 1.1

Relative Advantages of Holistic and Analytic Rubrics

In the *Rubric Sampler* on the CD, find at least one example of a holistic rubric and one example of an analytic rubric. Think about the following questions. Jot down your responses so that you can refer to them later.

- Which type would be better for an overall summation of level of achievement?

- Which type would be better for diagnosis and planning instruction?

- Which type would be better for helping students understand the components of quality and practice each separately?

- Which type would be better for a simple performance?

- Which type would be better for a complex performance?

Comparing Task-Specific and General Rubrics

Task-specific rubrics, unsurprisingly, are those specific to a single task. There is a unique scoring guide tailored to each individual task. *General* rubrics are those than can be used to judge quality across similar tasks. Examples are shown in Figure 1.2 and Table 1.2.

Notice that the task-specific rubric in Figure 1.2 can only be used to judge the performance on the plant experiment, while the general rubric in Table 1.2 can be used to evaluate the quality of any science experiment.

Figure 1.2 Example of a Task-Specific Rubric for a Science Experiment

Plant Experiment Scoring Guide

Experimental Design

3 = Plants are in separate pots; there are at least three different light and three different watering conditions.

2 = Either light conditions or water conditions vary, but not both.

1 = Neither amount of light nor amount of water vary.

Measurements

3 = All water measurements are within 1 ml.

2 = All except one or two water measurements are within 1 ml.

1 = More than 2 water measurements are different from the right answer by more than 1 ml.

Graph

3 = A line graph is used, the graph has a reasonable scale, labels are correct, and data is graphed accurately.

2 = The graph is a line graph, but the scale, labels, and/or accuracy could be better.

1 = Either a line graph is not used or the line graph makes little sense.

Conclusion/Discussion

3 = The conclusion clearly reflects the results and ties the results to the original hypothesis.

2 = There is a conclusion, but it either does not clearly reflect the results, or fails to connect the results convincingly to the original hypothesis.

1 = No conclusion is provided, or the conclusion is incomprehensible.

Table 1.2 Example of a General Rubric for a Science Experiment

This rubric for science experiments has four criteria: *Scientific Procedures and Reasoning*, *Strategies*, *Scientific Communication/Using Data*, and *Scientific Concepts and Related Content*. Scoring guides for two of the criteria appear here. The entire rubric can be found in Appendix C and on the accompanying CD.

Level	Scientific Procedures and Reasoning	Strategies
Novice	• Did not use appropriate scientific tools or technologies . . . to gather data . . .	• No evidence of a strategy or procedure, or used a strategy that did not bring about successful completion of task/investigation. • No evidence of scientific reasoning used. • There were so many errors in the process of investigation that the task could not be completed.
Apprentice	• Attempted to use appropriate tools and technologies . . . to gather data . . . but some information was inaccurate or incomplete.	• Used a strategy that was somewhat useful, leading to partial completion of the task/investigation. • Some evidence of scientific reasoning used. • Attempted but could not completely carry out testing a question, recording all data and stating conclusions.
Practitioner	• Effectively used some appropriate tools and technologies . . . to gather and analyze data, with only minor errors.	• Used a strategy that led to completion of the investigation/task. • Recorded all data. • Used effective scientific reasoning. • Framed or used testable questions, conducted experiment, and supported results with data.

Table 1.2 (Continued)

Expert	• Accurately and proficiently used all appropriate tools and technologies ... to gather and analyze data.	• Used a sophisticated strategy and revised strategy where appropriate to complete the task. • Employed refined and complex reasoning and demonstrated understanding of cause and effect. • Applied scientific method accurately: (framed testable questions, designed experiment, gathered and recorded data, analyzed data, and verified results).

Source: From "Exemplars Assessment Rubrics," retrieved from http://www.exemplars.com/resources/rubrics/science.html. Copyright © 2004 by Exemplars. Used with permission.

Activity 1.2

Relative Advantages of Task-Specific and General Rubrics

In the *Rubric Sampler* on the CD of sample rubrics, find at least one example of a task-specific rubric and one example of a general rubric. Think about the following questions. Jot down your responses so that you can refer to them later.

- Which type would be better for quick scoring?

- Which type would be better for helping students understand the components of quality and practice each separately?

- Which type would be better for tracking student progress over time and across different tasks?

When to Use the Various Types of Rubrics

We have some definite ideas on when to use each of these types of rubrics. But to have our recommendations make sense, we need to delve into the kinds of learning targets we are trying to assess.

Learning Targets

Learning targets are statements of what we want students to know and be able to do. These days, they are also called *content standards, benchmarks, indicators, goals, objectives, grade-level expectations*, and a variety of other things. We use the term *learning target* because it is neutral and can be used across terminology borders. Feel free, however, to substitute whatever term you use locally.

In our work, we designate four kinds of learning targets:

- *Knowledge*—both individual facts and a body of knowledge such as the carbon cycle

- *Reasoning proficiencies*—such as analysis, comparison, synthesis, inference, hypothesizing, problem solving, evaluative thinking, and critical thinking

- *Performance skills*—such as giving an oral presentation, speaking a foreign language, using equipment in the science lab or the mechanics shop, working in a group, operating a sewing machine, and playing a musical instrument

- *Creating products*—such as research reports, graphs, tables, maps, three-dimensional objects, visual artwork, and timelines

Examples of various kinds of learning targets are shown in Table 1.3.

Table 1.3 Examples of Each Kind of Learning Target

	Knowledge	Reasoning	Performance Skill	Product
Mathematics	Recognizes and describes patterns (NRC, p. 219)	Uses statistical methods to describe, analyze, evaluate, and make decisions (NRC, p. 219)	Measures length in metric and U.S. units (CKSD Gr. K–6 Math, p. 36)	Constructs bar graphs (CKSD Gr. K–6 Math, p. 38)
Language Arts (reading/ literature)	Recognizes similes, metaphors, and analogies (CKSD Gr. 7–10 Lang., p. 10)	Formulates questions, makes predictions, verifies and revises understanding while reading (CKSD Gr. 7–10 Lang., p. 41)	Reads aloud with fluency and expression (CKSD Gr. K–6 Lang., p. 32)	None
Physical Education	Understands long-term physiological benefits of regular participation in physical activity (CKSD PE, p. 46)	Analyzes fitness assessments to set personal fitness goals; strategizes ways to reach goals; evaluates activities (CKSD PE, p. 54)	Dribbles to keep the ball away from an opponent; passes and receives on the move (CKSD PE, p. 44)	Develops a personal health-related fitness plan (CKSD PE, p. 47)
Social Studies	Explains the important characteristics of U.S. citizenship (WA EALR: Civics)	Distinguishes between historical fact and opinion; compares and contrasts points of view from an historical event (CKSD Soc. St., p. 83)	Participates in civic discussions with the aim of solving current problems (WA EALR: Civics)	Creates a product that uses social studies content to support a thesis (WA EALR: Soc. St. Skills)

Table 1.3 (Continued)

Science	Knows that energy can be transformed between various forms (CKSD Sci., p. 7)	Examines data/results and proposes meaningful interpretation (CKSD Sci., p. 20)	Uses simple equipment and tools to gather data (CKSD Sci., p. 19)	Constructs physical models of familiar objects (CKSD Sci., p. 21)
Theater	Identifies elements of design in a given play (NT Gr. 6)	Compares and contrasts theater performances from various cultures and times using appropriate arts vocabulary (NT Gr. 5)	Demonstrates relationship and interactive responsibilities of the artist/performer and audience (WA EALR: Arts)	Creates a scripted scene based on improvised work (NT Gr. 5)
Spanish	Comprehends vocabulary (CKSD World Lang., p. 13)	Compares and contrasts cultural features from the U.S.A. and the Spanish-speaking world (CKSD World Lang., p. 13)	Pronounces correctly: vowel/consonant sounds; diphthongs (CKSD World Lang., p. 13)	Writes simple descriptions and narratives (CKSD World Lang., p. 13)

Source: Adapted from *Classroom Assessment* for *Student Learning: Doing It Right–Using It Well* (p. 63, Table 3.1) by R. J. Stiggins, J. Arter, J. Chappuis, & S. Chappuis, 2004, Portland, OR, Assessment Training Institute. Items are taken from the following sources. See the References for full citations: CKSD = Central Kitsap School District (1999–2002); NRC = National Research Council (1996); NT = North Thurston Public Schools (2001); WA EALR = *Washington State Essential Academic Learning Requirements* (Office of Superintendent of Public Instruction, 2004a–c).

Recommendations for When to Use Each Type of Rubric

There are two major things to think about when choosing a rubric type: the kind of learning target you are assessing, and how you will use the rubric—whether as an assessment *of* or *for* learning. A summary of our thoughts appears in Table 1.4. Compare our recommendations to your thoughts as you answered the questions in Activities 1.1 and 1.2.

Table 1.4 When to Use Different Kinds of Scoring Guides and Rubrics

	Large Scale[1]	Grading	Teacher Uses: Plan Instruction; Feedback to Students	Student Uses: Self-Assessment; Track Progress; Communicate
Knowledge— Specific Knowledge to Be Learned by All Students	Task specific	Task specific	Task specific	Task specific
Knowledge— Student Choice as to Knowledge to Be Demonstrated	Probably would never happen	General holistic	General holistic	General holistic
Reasoning Proficiencies, Performance Skills, Products	Task specific or general holistic	Task specific or general holistic unless the grading rubric is also used instruc-tionally	General analytic	General analytic

[1]Large-scale assessment takes place across classrooms using the same assessment materials at roughly the same time and under the same conditions, such as state tests.

First Consideration: Intended Use of the Rubric

General rubrics are better than task-specific scoring guides if the use is assessment *for* learning: helping students gain depth in their understanding of how to create a quality product or performance, self-assess and set goals for learning, track their own progress over time, and/or, communicate about their achievement growth with others.

Students do not learn the keys to quality problem solving, for example, by seeing task-specific scoring of individual mathematics problems. Consider the following task from a math assessment intended to measure problem-solving achievement:

Students were shown a picture of a complicated three-dimensional stack of blocks. (Some of the blocks could not be seen because of the two-dimensional rendering of the three-dimensional stack.) The task asked students to answer three questions:

Part A: How many blocks are in the stack?

Part B: How many blocks would be in a similar stack having 4 sides and a height of 6?

Part C: Write an equation for determining the number of blocks given any value of number of sides (X) and height (Y).

The answer in the task-specific scoring guide for Part B was, *Each side has 15 blocks; there are four sides, 15 X 4 = 60.* There is nothing in this statement, nor in any task-specific scoring guide, that will help students perform better on the next problem. Task-specific scoring is often suitable in a large-scale test setting, especially when raters need to work fast to minimize scoring costs and the purpose of the assessment is to generate an overall estimation of problem-solving ability. But, it isn't useful in the classroom when students are learning the nature of good mathematical problem solving so that they can apply that knowledge to the next problem.

Students learn what quality problem solving looks like through such statements as, "The way I worked the problem makes sense and is easy to follow," and, "I followed through with my strategy from beginning to end," coupled with examples that show what is meant. One study of the power of rubrics to help students learn resulted in this conclusion: "The influencing of instructional practices to date has been served most powerfully by generic rubrics" (Office of Educational Research and Improvement, 1997, p. xx). We maintain that this is true because general (generic) rubrics define successful attainment of the learning target, give students a vocabulary for talking about quality in general, and make it easier for them to generalize from one assessment to the next.

Second Consideration: Learning Target

Case 1: Assessing a Specific Body of Knowledge. Let's say that you want to find out if students have learned a particular concept or body of content. This would be a knowledge learning target, but it is beyond simple demonstration of knowledge of individual facts (in which case you wouldn't need a scoring guide at all because the best way to assess facts are multiple choice, true-false, matching, and short answer; see Stiggins, Arter, Chappuis, & Chappuis, 2004). For example, let's say that you want to see if students know all the steps in cell division in order, how supply and demand works, or the major causes of the Civil War and how they are related. So, you ask students to describe these things in writing—extended written response, or orally—extended oral response.

To score responses you decide how many points to assign to various parts of the answer. For example, in cell division you might assign five points to a response that gets all the steps right, and another five points if the steps are in the right order. This is task-specific scoring of knowledge when the goal is to see if the students learned this specific body of knowledge.

This is an acceptable use of task-specific scoring. The difference with this example of task-specific scoring and the example using the blocks is that here the goal is to see if students have acquired a specific body of knowledge. In the blocks example, the goal was to assess a reasoning proficiency—problem solving.

When determining if students have mastered a particular body of knowledge demonstrated through extended written response, use task-specific scoring. Do not use a task-specific scoring guide for reasoning proficiencies, performance skills, or products, especially when the purpose is assessment *for* learning.

A task-specific scoring guide that is appropriately designed to assess a specific body of knowledge is shown in Figure 1.3.

Case 2: Assessing a Body of Knowledge That Might Be Different Across Students. Sometimes you want students to acquire knowledge, but students may choose the particular topic they will study. For example, you're having students write a research paper on the Renaissance. They can choose to focus on art, science, a famous person, and so on. Through this research report you want students to practice research skills and writing as well as to gain expertise on a topic of their choice.

In this example, since each student might select a different topic, you can't use task-specific scoring because you would need a separate scoring guide for each topic. Instead, you would want a general rubric for content understanding that you could use across papers having different content. (Such a general conceptual understanding rubric appears in the *Rubric Sampler* on the CD.) Other examples of when you might want to use a general conceptual understanding rubric are as follows:

- Students will use their knowledge of health and fitness to write a personal fitness plan, but because the plan is tailored to themselves, they have a choice of what specific knowledge to demonstrate.

- Students will write a research paper on how change occurs, but they can choose any topic from personal change to change in scientific ideas.

- Students select different pieces of work to put into their portfolios to illustrate their ability to solve problems.

Figure 1.3 Appropriate Use of Task-Specific Scoring to Assess Knowledge-Level Learning Targets

Task

We have been studying the importance of the carbon cycle and how it works. Based on your understanding of the carbon cycle, please describe why we need to know about it and how it works. Be sure to include the following:

- Why it is important to understand the carbon cycle: 5 points

- The four major places (reservoirs) we studied where carbon is stored: 4 points

- At least six ways that carbon gets transferred from one place to another: 6 points

Task-Specific Scoring Guide

Why it is important to understand the carbon cycle. One point for any five of the following:

- Carbon is stored in the atmosphere in the form of carbon dioxide.

- Carbon dioxide in the atmosphere can cause greenhouse warming of the planet.

- In recent times geologically, carbon has stayed in balance: the amount of carbon being added to the atmosphere is balanced by the amount of carbon lost from the atmosphere.

- A balanced carbon cycle keeps the planet from warming up or cooling down.

- Humans could cause this system to become unbalanced through burning fossil fuels and from other activities.

- A carbon cycle out of balance could add more carbon to the atmosphere than is being removed through natural means and could lead to global warming.

- The extent to which global warming is actually occurring is currently being researched and debated among scientists.

The major reservoirs of carbon. One point for each of the following:
atmosphere, oceans, land/sediments, and plants/animals.

How carbon moves from one place to another. One point for any six of the following:

- Carbon moves from the atmosphere to plants through photosynthesis.

- Carbon moves from the atmosphere to oceans by dissolving in places it is cold.

- Carbon moves from the oceans to the atmosphere by evaporation where it is hot.

- Carbon moves from plant/animals to the atmosphere through breathing/respiration.

- Carbon moves from land to the atmosphere through
  a. Fires
  b. Volcanic eruptions
  c. Burning fossil fuels

- Carbon moves from the land into the oceans through erosion.

- Carbon moves from plants/animals to the ground/sediments through decay.

Case 3: Assessing Both Knowledge and a Reasoning Proficiency, a Performance Skill, or a Product. What about the situation where you both want to see if students have learned a specific body of knowledge and also want to determine whether they can reason using that knowledge? In this case the scoring and general rubric(s) might have both task-specific and general portions. For example, consider critiquing art. To critique art students might need to know both art terminology and concepts such as *composition, perspective,* and *shading*, and the features of art of a particular era and location. The critique itself involves drawing on knowledge to determine and explain what the artist was attempting to accomplish and how well she accomplished it. In this case you might have both a task-specific portion of the rubric for determining content knowledge and a general rubric for critique.

Summary.

- Don't use rubrics at all if you want to assess independent pieces of knowledge. Assess these with multiple-choice, true-false, matching, or short answer items.

- Use task-specific scoring when you ask students for an extended written or oral response to see how well they understand a specific body of information and how it works together.

- Use a general conceptual understanding rubric when you want to see how well students understand a body of information, but selection of information might vary among students.

- Use general rubrics for reasoning, performance skill, and product learning targets, such as making inferences, playing a musical instrument, planning an experiment, writing a piece of music, writing a research report, or writing a lab report.

Third Consideration: Learning Target Complexity

So, you've decided on a general rubric because you are planning to use it to help students learn how to reason well, perform skillfully, or create a quality product. The next decision is, is your rubric to be holistic or analytic?

In the classroom, it makes sense to use holistic scoring guides when the reasoning, performance skill, or product target seems to have only a single dimension of quality. For example, we suspect that a single, holistic rubric can serve to define reasoning proficiencies such as analyzing, comparing, and classifying. A holistic rubric might also be sufficient, as noted previously, for general conceptual understanding.

In the classroom, use analytic scoring guides when the reasoning, performance skill, or product target has several dimensions of quality and it would be useful for students to have each defined separately. For example, good writing depends on clearly focused ideas, organization that supports the ideas, appropriate voice, effective word choice, fluent sentences, and correct writing conventions. High-quality responses to open-ended mathematics problems depend on understanding the problem, employing appropriate problem-solving strategies, calculating accurately, and clearly communicating what was done and why it was done. (Rubrics for writing and mathematics problem solving appear in the *Rubric Sampler* on the CD.)

Here is what Donald Graves (1983) says about the usefulness during learning of breaking performance into manageable traits:

> *One of the best examples of good teaching I have ever encountered was with a golf professional. On my first lesson, he said, "Here is a bucket of balls . . . hit 'em." A few minutes later he wandered back and quietly said, "Keep hitting them, only this time keep your head down, eye on the ball." By the next bucket of balls he had introduced one more skill for the day . . . no more. Before a few weeks were out, he had quietly attended to my feet, grip, shoulder level,*

and follow through. A few years later I realized with a start that every single one of my problems was visible on the first lesson. If I had attended to all of them that first day, I would probably have missed the ball entirely and resigned in disgust from ever playing golf again. (n.p.)

When searching for a rubric to measure reasoning proficiencies, performance skills, or products, you won't necessarily know ahead of time which rubric type you are looking for. The decision becomes clear during the process of begging, borrowing, and stealing—and, if absolutely necessary, developing your own—rubrics. You look to see what others recommend or what emerges through the development process.

Fourth Consideration: Efficiency

There's no doubt, task-specific and general, holistic rubrics are quicker to learn and use than analytic rubrics if the only goal is to quickly obtain information on the overall learning status of students—assessment *of* learning. Such might be the case with state or provincial assessments and, in the classroom, grading when there is *lots* of student work to evaluate.

But, if we want to use rubrics at all as assessments *for* learning, speed is probably not the major consideration; adequate description of the components of quality is. Therefore, a general, analytic rubric is better.

Focus on General Rubrics

The bottom line is that all types of scoring guides are useful if you attend to the learning target to be assessed and the purpose for the assessment. However, do not use a task-specific rubric when a general rubric would better fit the learning target and purpose, and do not use a holistic rubric when an analytic one would be a better fit.

In this book we will focus on general rubrics for reasoning proficiencies, performance skill, and product learning targets. For more information on developing task-specific rubrics see Stiggins et al. (2004), Chapters 6 and 7.

Activity 1.3

Apply This Information to Your Own Rubrics, Part 1

Think about the reasoning, performance skill, and product development learning targets you have for students. Of all these possible learning targets, choose the one or two for which it would benefit students (and yourself) the most to have a rubric. To identify them, determine those targets students have the most problems with or the most questions about, or those where you encounter the most difficulty when grading.

Activity 1.4

Apply This Information to Your Own Rubrics, Part 2

1. Find several examples of rubrics you have used. Classify each as task specific, general holistic, or general analytic.

2. What type of learning target is each rubric attempting to measure—knowledge, reasoning, performance skill, or product?

3. How do you use each scoring guide—to judge level of proficiency, to grade, to communicate quality to students, to offer feedback to students, to allow students to self-assess?

4. How well does the rubric type match up to the learning target and intended use? Does anything need adjusting?

The Path Ahead: Book Content

Several conditions are essential for rubrics to work well in helping teachers teach and students learn. First, we, the teachers, need a clear vision ourselves of the features, dimensions, and indicators of a quality product or performance. Second, we need to communicate this vision to students effectively, so that they, too, develop the ability to judge quality.

This book will address both issues. Chapters 2 and 3 address how to obtain a clear vision in our own minds of the dimensions of quality work. Chapter 2 talks about the features of rubrics that make them most productive as instructional tools, and Chapter 3 details procedures for developing these high-quality rubrics. Chapter 6 delves into procedures for using rubrics with students as assessment *for* learning to increase achievement. For examples of assessment *for* learning applications using other types of assessment, see Stiggins et al., 2004.

The remaining chapters address other aspects of using rubrics well. Chapter 4 discusses performance task quality. The task has to elicit the correct performance on the part of students, or you won't be able to assess student mastery regardless of the quality of the rubric. The success of using rubrics also depends on the quality of the assignments and tasks that students are to perform.

Chapter 5 tackles the difficult but crucial question of how to convert rubric scores to grades in a way that most accurately reflects student achievement at the time the grade is given, while avoiding unintended negative consequences of the conflict between using rubrics for learning and using them for grading.

Finally, Chapter 7 presents ideas on how to explain rubrics to parents so that they, too, can participate with their children in exploring the nature of quality work.

It is difficult to discuss rubrics in depth without concrete examples for discussion. A rubric sampler, provided on the accompanying CD, includes rubrics for various grade levels and subject matter areas representing a continuum of quality ranging from strong to weak. A table of contents for the *Rubric Sampler* appears in Appendix B.

We will also incorporate boxed features into the text containing extra information that (1) we want to draw attention to (*Misconception Alert*); (2) provides a depth of detail beyond that which might be of interest to the general reader (*For the Connoisseur*), or (3) we feel is important, but that seems to be outside of the main points in the text (*Variation on the Theme*).

Summary

1. There is no Central Bureau for Consistent Terminology When Using Rubrics. We use the following definitions: A *rubric* occurs when performance criteria are written down and levels are defined. A *scoring guide* is the same thing as a *rubric*. *Criteria* (also called *traits*) are the major dimensions of work that are important.

2. Rubrics define the features of work that constitute quality. They are the mechanism for judging the quality of student work.

3. Rubrics help teachers clarify for themselves what ambiguous learning targets look like. They help students do the same.

4. There is a body of research showing that, if done well, using rubrics with students (assessment *for* learning) can have a dramatic impact on student learning.

5. All assessments in which students construct a response rather than choosing a response from a list require a scoring guide of some sort.

6. All decisions about which rubric to use depend on the answers to two questions: (1) What is the purpose for the assessment? (2) What learning targets will the assessment measure?

7. There are two basic purposes for using rubrics: *Assessment* of *learning* seeks to specify student achievement as of a point in time, such as grading. *Assessment* for *learning* occurs when assessment results, processes, or products are used to boost student learning prior to the assessment *of* learning event. Rubrics are useful tools for both, but different purposes might require different types of rubrics.

8. Different types of rubrics serve different purposes. Task-specific scoring guides can only be used with a single task. General rubrics can be used to assess the same proficiency across a variety of similar tasks. Holistic rubrics result in a single, overall judgment for an entire performance or product. Analytic rubrics allow you to break a complex performance into parts and evaluate each part separately.

9. All types of rubrics and scoring guides are viable options depending on intended use and kind of learning target (knowledge, reasoning, performance skill, and product). In general,

   - Use task-specific scoring guides for knowledge-level learning targets.

   - Use general rubrics for reasoning, performance skill, and product types of learning targets.

   - Use holistic rubrics for speed scoring to grade (assessment *of* learning), to get a general overall look at a group, or when the learning target is not complex enough to require more than a single criterion.

   - Use analytic rubrics for complex performances or products, especially when you want to use the rubric to help plan instruction or provide descriptive feedback to students, or when you plan to use the rubric instructionally with students (assessment *for* learning).

chapter

$$[\ 2\ ]$$

What Does a Good Rubric Look Like?

What words could I use to explain to Larry and his mother that there
was more to a 6 than meeting the criteria that were originally stated?
How could I explain that Larry's paper lacked "quality?"

—J. Babb

"Finding the Right Words," in J. H. Shulman, A. Whittaker, & M. Lew (Eds.),
Using Assessments to Teach for Understanding, New York: Teachers College Press, 2002, p. 90

Obviously, the teacher quoted in this chapter's epigraph was not using a rubric that possessed the descriptive power needed to communicate the subtle features that created her definition of a quality paper. This chapter explores the characteristics of rubrics that allow them to define clearly what quality looks like, so that teachers *are* able to explain "quality" to all who need to know.

Features of a Good-Quality Rubric

What makes a good rubric? How do we know one when we see it? If we type "rubric" into any Internet search engine, we get from 1,000,000 to 13,000,000 hits. How do we know which to choose? It's impossible to answer these questions without first considering how we want to use rubrics in the classroom. In Chapter 1, we noted the following ways to use rubrics:

- Help students understand what is wanted on an assignment.
- Help students understand what a quality performance or product looks like.
- Help students understand what they did well and what to do differently next time.
- Enable students to self-assess.
- Help teachers plan instruction.
- Help teachers grade consistently.
- Help teachers have sound justifications for grades.
- Help teachers and students communicate with parents.

You will notice that this list includes both assessment *for* and assessment *of* learning uses. Both are helpful in the classroom. To be able to fulfill these uses, rubrics must

- Be understandable
- Be aligned with standards
- Be illustrated with samples of student work
- Be concise
- Be stated in a way students can understand
- Be easy to use
- Be worded in a positive manner
- Match the assignment/task
- Define various levels of performance
- Include the same features across various levels of performance

Teachers and researchers generally agree on the features of high-quality rubrics (Johnson, 1996; Moskal, 2000; Perlman, 2004; Popham, 2002; Rohrmann, 2003; Tierney & Simon, 2004). From our own experience (bolstered by these sources and work with teachers and students) we have developed a *Rubric for Rubrics*. Figure 2.1 shows a summary. The entire *Rubric for Rubrics* appears in Appendix A and on the accompanying CD.

We developed the *Rubric for Rubrics* to evaluate rubrics for use in the classroom, not for use with large-scale assessments such as state or provincial assessments. Although many features of quality would be the same for both uses, large-scale rubrics often end up with features that would be counterproductive in a rubric intended for classroom use. For example, developers of rubrics for large-scale uses frequently emphasize a quick, overall picture of student performance—no detail. Rubrics used in the classroom, on the other hand, often need to provide detailed diagnostic information to inform day-to-day instructional decisions.

The *Rubric for Rubrics* is intended to be used with general, not task-specific, rubrics. We emphasize general rubrics because they help define those learning targets often least clear in curriculum documents (such as assessing reasoning proficiencies,

Figure 2.1 **Rubric for Rubrics** *Summary*

---

1. **Coverage/Organization:** What counts in a student's work?

   A. **Covers the Right Content.** Does the rubric cover everything of importance? Does it leave out unimportant things?

   - Does the content of the rubric represent the best thinking in the field about what it means to perform well on the skill or product under consideration?

   - Does the content of the rubric align directly with the content standards or learning targets it is intended to assess?

   - Does the content have the "ring of truth"—does your experience as a teacher confirm that the content is truly what you *do* look for when you evaluate the quality of student work or performance?

   B. **Criteria Are Well Organized.** Is the rubric divided into easily understandable chunks (criteria), as needed?

   - Is the number of criteria appropriate for the complexity of the learning target?

   - Are the descriptors for each criterion organized well?

   - Does the relative emphasis among criteria represent their relative importance?

   - Is the contribution of each criterion clear with minimal overlap among them?

   C. **Number of Levels Fits Targets and Uses.** Is the number of levels appropriate for the intended learning target and use? Can users distinguish among the levels?

2. **Clarity:** Does everyone understand what is meant?

   A. **Levels Defined Well.** Is each level of the rubric clearly defined?

   - Do definitions rely on descriptive words and phrases rather than on (1) nonspecific words such as *"excellent"* and *"thorough,"* or (2) counting the number or frequency of something? *Plusses:* examples of student work at each level for all criteria, and student-friendly versions.

   - Would two independent raters, with training, give the same rating to the same product or performance?

   - Is wording descriptive, not evaluative?

   B. **Levels Parallel.** Are the levels of the rubric parallel in content?

   - If a feature is mentioned at one level, is it also mentioned at all the other levels?

---

performance skills, or products). Also, they can be given to students in advance of the assessment to practice with.

The *Rubric for Rubrics* has two criteria—*Coverage/ Organization* and *Clarity*. We discuss each criterion first using the summary in Figure 2.1. We then explore each in more detail using the complete *Rubric for Rubrics* in Appendix A.

Understanding *Rubric for Rubrics* Criterion 1: *Coverage/ Organization*

The *content* of a classroom rubric defines what to look for in a student's product or performance to determine its quality: what will "count." Teachers and students use this content to determine what they must do to succeed. What students see is what you'll get.

Indicator 1A: Covers the Right Content

The first thing to think about is the extent to which the rubric covers all the important features of work or performance that really do add to quality and leaves out features that do not relate to the learning target at hand, or that are not important. For example, the rubric for a lab report *would* include flow—the entire report relates to the original hypothesis and is not filled with irrelevant details—and the nature and sufficiency of the manner in which results are displayed. Such a rubric *would not* include length. Indicators of having the right content include the following:

- The content of the rubric represents the best thinking in the field about what it means to perform well on the skill or product under consideration.

- The content of the rubric aligns with the content standards and learning targets it is intended to measure.

- The content of the rubric sounds right to you. It represents what you really *do* look for. In fact, it supports and extends your understanding about what you should look for when evaluating student work.

Please note that you can accurately judge the soundness of a rubric's content coverage only if you are well versed in the content domain.

Indicator 1B: Criteria Are Well Organized

The list of features that describe quality should be as concise as possible and organized into a usable form. This often involves identifying and grouping similar features into criteria and making sure that the relative importance given to each criterion represents its relative contribution to the quality of the product or performance as a whole.

Indicator 1C: Number of Levels Fits Targets and Uses

Finally, the number of levels needs to be appropriate for the intended learning target and your use of the rubric. Can users distinguish among the levels? Do the number of levels allow you to distinguish different levels of quality so that you (or the students themselves) can adequately track student progress?

Strong Example of Coverage/Organization: 6 + 1 Trait™ Writing Assessment Scoring Guide

Consider the *6 + 1 Trait™ Writing Assessment Scoring Guide*, found in Appendix C and on the CD (which we will also refer to here as the *6-Trait* writing rubric). This rubric includes six criteria (which the authors call *traits*): *Ideas, Organization, Voice, Word Choice, Sentence Fluency*, and *Conventions* (spelling, grammar, capitalization, and punctuation). (Note that the rubric also contains a seventh, optional, criterion—*Presentation*—which we do not address in this book.) This rubric content represents current expert thinking in the field, aligns closely with many content standards documents, and has the ring of truth to teachers (*Rubric for Rubrics* indicator 1A).

Further, the *6-Trait* writing rubric is divided into useful and understandable criteria (*Rubric for Rubrics* indicator 1B) so that each component that contributes to quality writing can be

---

Misconception Alert
Shouldn't We Always Use an Even Number of Levels?

Some people advocate four or six levels because they feel that (1) with five levels, it is too tempting to equate each level to a letter grade, and (2) with three levels, the middle point can become a dumping ground for all but the strongest and weakest work. We hold that the number of levels depends on the learning target being assessed and the use of the rubric. What is important is a good rationale for the number of levels.

---

analyzed, taught, and evaluated separately. The contribution of each criterion to the whole is clear.

Additionally, the number of criteria is appropriate for the complexity of the learning target (*Rubric for Rubrics* indicator 1B). Writing *is* complicated. To make the components that contribute to quality clear to students, it is useful to define them separately. We have seen writing rubrics with three criteria— *Ideas/Organization*, *Style* (voice, word choice, and sentence fluency), and *Conventions*. These are combined in this fashion because the users feel that ideas and structure are so interwoven that it is difficult to judge them separately; likewise for the elements of style. We have also seen writing rubrics with eight criteria—*Ideas*, *Organization*, *Voice*, *Word Choice*, *Sentence Fluency*, *Spelling*, *Grammar*, and *Punctuation/ Capitalization*. This is done so that each component of conventions can be examined separately. None of these divisions is inherently superior; your choice depends on the use you intend to make of the assessment information.

With respect to number of levels (*Rubric for Rubrics* indicator 1C), what is important is that there is a good rationale. The *6-Trait* writing rubric has such a rationale. It has five levels of quality; levels 1, 3, and 5 are defined. Level 2 is a balance of levels 1 and 3; level 4 is a balance of levels 3 and 5. Level 5 means "in control of this trait." Level 3 means "gaining control of this trait." Level 1 means "just beginning to understand what is required for this trait."

Medium Quality Example of Coverage/Organization: Job Application Letter Scoring Guide

An example of a rubric for a job application letter appears in Figure 2.2. What do you see as its strengths and weaknesses on the *Rubric for Rubrics* criterion of *Coverage/Organization?*

Here's what we notice with respect to the first indicator, *A. Covers the Right Content.* The rubric seems to include many features of a good job application letter. We don't have this teacher's content standards in front of us, so we can't judge the extent to which the features on the rubric align with content standards. Even so, it doesn't quite have the "ring of truth"—do features 15–20 cover the only possible content that such a letter should have? Should there be more about organization? Might the tone of the letter also be important? (Note also that features 5 and 12 are duplicates. A student thus would gain or lose credit twice for the same feature of the work. A strong rubric avoids redundancy.)

With reference to the second indicator, *B. Criteria Are Well Organized,* the criteria seem out of balance; students would get many more points for format than for content. Also, 28 features seem like a lot to rate. Might it be more practical and conceptually clear to condense these features into more comprehensive criteria, such as the following 4? Using this condensed rubric would mean that each job application letter would get 4 ratings instead of 28.

1. *Content/Organization.* Does the content of the letter touch on all important points (features 15–20 in Figure 2.2)? Is the content organized in such a way that the reader is led easily from beginning to end? (The latter is not really addressed in the current rubric.)

Figure 2.2 Job Application Letter Scoring Guide

Each of the following is to be rated on a scale from 1 to 3.			
Letter includes applicant's			
1. Street address			
2. City, state, zip			
3. Date written out			
4. Followed by three blank lines			
5. The salutation includes addressee's name			
6. Full name of person to receive letter			
7. Title of person if known			
8. Name of company			
9. Address			
10. City, state, zip			
11. Followed by a double space			
12. Salutation includes addressee's name			
13. Followed by a ":"			
14. Followed by a double space			
Letter			
15. Opens with a strong, positive statement about the applicant or his qualifications or			
16. Opens with a statement naming a person known by the addressee who advised the applicant of the available position			
17. Highlights the best items from applicant's background which directly qualifies her for the job			
18. States why the applicant wants to work for this organization			
19. Requests an interview			
20. Suggests how the applicant will follow up or where he can be reached to schedule an interview			
21. Includes a proper closing followed by a comma			
22. Closing is followed by four hard returns			
23. Applicant's full real name is typed below the closing			
24. Applicant signs the letter in ink between the closing and her name			
25. Letter is one page			
26. Sentences and paragraphs are short and easy to read			
27. No misspelled words or grammar errors			
28. Printed on high-quality paper			

Source: Adapted from a rubric developed by Anna Lipski, Grossmont High School, La Mesa, CA, n.d. Adapted with permission.

2. *Tone/Word Choice.* Is the tone of the letter suited to the intended audience and purpose? Do the words used communicate meaning precisely? (These points do not appear in the current rubric.)

3. *Sentences/Conventions.* Are the sentences and paragraphs easy to read? Are all words spelled correctly? Is the letter grammatically correct? Are punctuation and capitalization correct? (Currently only features 26 and 27 address this criterion.)

4. *Format/Presentation.* Does the letter adhere to business format? Does it look professional? This combines features 1–14, 21–25, and 28 into one criterion. Would this provide a better balance of format with content? (Note: Students could use a checklist to supplement this criterion, so that they remember all the formatting details.)

We note the following with respect to the third indicator, *C. Number of Levels Fits Targets and Uses.* Three levels of quality seem appropriate for some features. But some of the features are simply either present or absent. It would be difficult to rate such features as "followed by a ':'" (Item 13) on a three-point scale—it's either there or it's not. A checklist would be a better choice to track presence or absence of many format features. Then, an overall score could be given to format—rubric criterion 4 in our condensed list.

Understanding *Rubric for Rubrics* Criterion 2: *Clarity*

A classroom rubric is *clear* to the extent that teachers, students, and others are likely to interpret the statements and terms in the rubric the same way. A rubric can be strong on the criterion of *Coverage/Organization* but weak on the criterion of *Clarity*—the rubric seems to cover the important dimensions of performance, but doesn't describe them very well. Likewise, a rubric can be strong on the criterion of *Clarity,* but weak on the criterion of *Coverage/Organization*—it's very clear what the rubric means, but it is not focused on the right criteria.

Indicator 2A: Levels Defined

The key with clarity is to define levels so transparently that students (and teachers) can see precisely what features of work cause people to agree that work is strong, medium, or weak. The instructional usefulness of any rubric depends on the clarity of level descriptions.

Misconception Alert
Are We Assessing the Targets or the Task?

Consider two performance assessments:

1. A primary teacher is assessing student *concepts of print* by asking students to prepare a book cover.

2. A middle-school history teacher is assessing student *ability to make a map* by asking them to make a map.

Should the scoring guide for the book cover include features of the book cover itself, such as neatness and colorfulness? We think it should stick to concepts of print because the product—the book cover—is just the context for demonstrating achievement of the learning targets, in this case concepts of print. The scoring guide for the map, on the other hand, should consist of features of the map itself—map key, accurate details, and proportional distances, for example—because these *are* the learning targets.

Include on the rubric features of the product to be created by students only when the product *is* the target of the assessment. Do not include on the rubric features of the product to be created by students if the task is merely the *context* for demonstrating mastery of the target. Here's why: If you were to record a score in your gradebook for "book cover" and this score included neatness and colorfulness as well as concepts of print, that score would lose its meaning *vis à vis* concepts of print.

Read the questions referring to *Clarity* in Figure 2.1. Teachers generally agree these things are important. However, our objection to simply counting number or frequency may require explanation. Are five weak references on a research report better than three strong ones? Does an introductory paragraph need a specific number of sentences to be effective at drawing the reader in and setting up the topic? Quantity and quality are not always synonymous.

Counts are appropriate for certain criteria. For instance, students might monitor the frequency or consistency with which they adhere to various classroom rules, such as taking out needed materials or cleaning up a work area before being asked. Some academic learning targets might be monitored through use of counts, such as errors in oral reading or number of out-of-tune notes in a musical performance.

But, for most criteria, quality is not the same as quantity. If counts are used, make sure that counting *is* the best indicator of quality.

Indicator 2B: Levels Parallel

Rubrics should include a parallel feature of work on each level. For example, if you find that a rubric for playing the violin contains "lackadaisical bowing" as one descriptor of a middle-level performance, then a statement about the quality of the bowing must be included at the strong and weak levels as well. If the descriptor is not referred to at other levels, the levels are not parallel.

Strong Example of Clarity: 6 + 1 Trait™ Writing Assessment Scoring Guide

How clear is the *6-Trait* writing rubric? With respect to the first indicator, *A. Levels Defined,* the rubric attempts to be very descriptive in order to allow the user to match its words and phrases to work at hand. Consider the phrases under level 5 of the trait of *Organization:* "an inviting introduction draws the reader in"; "details seem to fit where they're placed"; "the writer knows when to slow down and elaborate, and when to pick up the pace and move on." Compare these to statements at level 1: "there is no real lead to set up what follows"; "sequencing needs lots and lots of work"; "pacing feels awkward; the writer slows to a crawl when the reader wants to get on with it, and vice versa."

Do these descriptive phrases take all the doubt out of a level determination? No. But, they are a long way from such vague words as *excellent* and *weak*. We know through research on this rubric that it is possible to obtain agreement rates between raters of 95 percent direct agreement and of above 99 percent within one point.

With respect to the second indicator: *B. Levels Parallel,* descriptors in the *6-Trait* writing rubric are strictly parallel in structure, as shown in the descriptors from the trait of *Organization* given previously.

Finally, the *6-Trait* writing rubric also has a student-friendly version, simplified yet equally clear (which also appears on the CD).

Weak Quality Example of Clarity: Job Application Letter Scoring Guide

As you examined the *Job Application Letter* rubric (Figure 2.2) for the *Rubric for Rubrics* criterion of *Coverage/Organization*, you also may have noticed some issues regarding *Clarity*.

Although it is fairly clear what each of the numbered features means, there is no description of levels. This is a moot point for features better assessed with a checklist—there is no need to define levels of quality because the feature is either present or absent. Other features, such as "opens with a strong, positive statement," do require judgment of levels of quality, but the only definition for those levels is *3, 2,* or *1*. This rubric is therefore weak on the criterion of *Clarity*.

Practicing with the Whole *Rubric for Rubrics*

The *Rubric for Rubrics* needs to adhere to its own criteria. One of the criteria is building clarity through examination of samples. This section attempts to practice what we preach: for each *Rubric for Rubrics* criterion and indicator we present strong, medium, and weak examples of classroom rubrics. You may not need to review every example with the same level of attention. You may just want to familiarize yourself with the *Rubric for Rubrics*'s general shape and content so you can retrieve information when you need to apply it to your own rubrics.

Misconception Alert

Shouldn't the Rubric Fit on One Page?

Whether a rubric should fit on one page depends on the use to which it will be put and the complexity of the learning target being captured. The *6-Trait* writing rubric, for example, fits on seven pages—one for each trait. Each trait needs enough descriptive detail so that teachers can be consistent in judging quality and students can understand what the trait means. Could it be more concise? Maybe. But we don't think it could be reduced to one page.

Keep the following two points in mind. First, you don't have to evaluate all criteria for every piece of work. This is especially true during learning. Evaluating criteria separately can often give you a better picture of student achievement and can give students focused feedback to use when improving their work.

Second, once you internalize the rubric you can put a brief version on a single page (or less) as a reminder, keeping the whole rubric handy in case questions arise.

Conciseness must not trump clarity in a rubric.

If you are reading this book because you are engaged in a formal rubric project, such as when developing your own, you might want to explore the examples in more depth to capture the nuances of quality.

Misconception Alert
Do Rubrics Limit Creativity?

Sometimes you may think, "If I specify exactly what a good product or performance looks like, won't I dampen individuality? Won't I cause all student work to look alike? How do I avoid restricting creativity?" Sometimes this manifests itself when you have to rate a performance low based on a rubric's wording when you feel the performance is actually good (or vice versa). When either of these happen, it's time to revise the rubric. Rubrics should not restrict students into a single mold of quality.

As an example, an earlier version of the *6-Trait* writing rubric contained the trait *Sentence Correctness*—sentences needed to be complete (although being varied and tailored to the audience was also good). This trait, though important, sometimes led to an unjustifiable low rating when students used sentence fragments well. On review, the rubric's authors decided that being in control of sentence structure should be what defined quality. *Being in control* means that students can craft sentences to support the ideas in the writing and select a structure that suits the audience, topic, and purpose for writing. Sometimes short, choppy, and fragmented works. Sometimes long, fluid, and complete is a better approach. Now the trait is called *Sentence Fluency*.

Here's another example: Consider a requirement that a poster have at least three colors to be judged effective. Why three? Can't a perfectly effective poster be black and white? Wouldn't it better to say "the poster's presentation should enhance the ideas and catch the viewer's attention"? There are many ways to accomplish this apart from number of colors.

You may wish at this point to print the *Rubric for Rubrics* from the CD, or make a copy of Appendix A. We'll be using its wording to discuss levels of quality in our examples; our explanations will be clearer if you have the *Rubric for Rubrics* in front of you.

The *Rubric for Rubrics* has the following structure:

1. Subheads under each criterion are *indicators*, and the subsequent numbered items are *descriptors*. An indicator, for example is, "Covers the right content." A descriptor for that indicator is, "The content of the rubric represents the best thinking in the field . . ."

2. The descriptors under each indicator are not meant to function as a checklist. Rather, they are meant to help the user determine the level of quality of the classroom rubric under consideration. Not everything has to be present (or missing) for the classroom rubric to be judged as meeting a particular level of quality. Ask yourself, "Which level of descriptors best describes the rubric I'm considering?"

3. An odd number of levels is used because the middle level represents a balance of strengths and weaknesses. It would take some work to fine tune a classroom rubric at the Medium level, but it probably is worth the effort.

4. A Strong score doesn't necessarily mean that the classroom rubric under consideration is perfect; rather, it means that it would require very little work to get it ready for use. A Weak score means that the classroom rubric needs so much work that it probably isn't worth the effort—it's time to find another one. It might even be easier to begin from scratch.

5. A Medium score does not mean *average*. This is a criterion-referenced scale, not a norm-referenced one. It is meant to describe levels of quality in a classroom rubric, not to compare those currently available. It could be that the typical currently available classroom rubric is closer to Weak than to Medium.

6. Although three levels are defined, it is in fact a *five-level* scale. Think of level 4 as a combination of characteristics from levels 5 and 3. Likewise, level 2 combines characteristics from levels 3 and 1.

As noted, in the following discussion we will be using terminology from the *Rubric for Rubrics* to describe elements of our examples. We will also call the rubrics being analyzed *classroom rubrics* to distinguish them from the *Rubric for Rubrics*.

Rubric for Rubrics Criterion 1: Coverage/Organization

Look at the *Rubric for Rubrics* criterion of *Coverage/ Organization*. Begin by reading the indicators and descriptors for the high level, *5—Strong*. Highlight any words or phrases that jump out at you as particularly indicating a strong performance. Then do the same for the low level, *1—Weak*, and finally for the middle level, *3—Medium*. (We recommend reading the rubric in this order because it is easier then to distinguish the extremes and see Medium as a balance of Strong and Weak.)

Indicator A: Covers the Right Content

The first indicator is *content*—the classroom rubric includes all important content and excludes irrelevant features. Content is actually the most important indicator. If a rubric does not cover the right features, at least at the Medium level, then it is useless to examine it on the other criteria and indicators.

Strong. Several classroom rubrics in Appendix C are Strong for this first criterion. We have already examined the *6 + 1 Trait™ Writing Assessment Scoring Guide*. In Appendix C also find the rubric *Mathematical Problem Solving: A Three-Trait Model, Adult Version* from Central Kitsap School District, and the *General Science Rubric*. They cover important features of performance, and they align to the content standards of the organizations that developed them. The content of each classroom rubric has the "ring of truth." One or more of these rubrics might need some work on one or more of the other indicators, but we judge their content to be Strong.

Medium. We have already discussed one example where some important features of performance were left out—the *Job Application Letter Scoring Guide* (Figure 2.2) left out organization and tone/word choice.

Medium. Consider the rubric *Middle School Oral Presentation* in Table 2.1. The criteria *Organization* and *Delivery* are represented on many good rubrics for evaluating an oral presentation; they are considered important to effectiveness.

In the *Middle School* rubric the criterion of *Delivery* includes many important features of an oral presentation, But, there are some features of sound *Delivery* that are not here: enunciation, pace, and absence of disfluencies, for example.

There are also two criteria, frequently on oral presentation rubrics, that are missing here: *Content* and *Language Use*. *Language Use* covers such features as the student's choice of words and using language that the listeners will understand. *Content* includes such things as completeness and accuracy. That these criteria are missing here is not automatically a problem; remember it is the learning targets you intend to assess that guide your decision about whether the rubric covers the right content. In the case of this rubric, without knowing the learning targets the teacher had in mind, it is difficult to judge. The teacher, for example, may have wanted to focus only on eye contact and volume for the criterion *Delivery*. It just needs to be clear that this rubric doesn't define the domain of *Delivery*.

Weak. Consider the Oregon Trail performance task and associated rubric in Figure 2.3. The learning targets are not stated and it is difficult to determine what they are from reading the task and rubric. From the task it seems that knowledge about the trip westward on the Oregon Trail will be assessed. But this is not what is represented on the rubric. The rubric assesses attractiveness of the map, creation of a diary with enough entries, readability, and finishing the project on time.

Table 2.1 *Middle School Oral Presentation*

Criterion	Proficient	Developing	Beginning
Organization	Introduction sets up topic	Recognizable introduction; may not catch audience interest	No discernable introduction
	All parts of presentation clearly related to the topic		Presentation includes seemingly extraneous information, with no attempt to help audience connect it to the topic
	Ideas and information presented with logical sequence	Most ideas and information in logical sequence; some parts may not fit where they are placed	Ideas and information presented in random, disconnected order
	Use of visual aids emphasizes main points and enhances message	Visual aids all relate to the topic and do not distract attention from message	Visual aids are unrelated to topic and/or distract attention from message
	Conclusion summarizes presentation	Recognizable conclusion; may be only a restatement of main points	Presentation just ends; no discernable conclusion
	Is able to answer audience's questions		
Delivery	Projects a sense of confidence; seems friendly	Demeanor does not distract from the presentation; does not seem afraid	Projects a sense of discomfort and lack of confidence; seems stiff
	Eye contact is maintained with audience throughout presentation		Does not look at audience
	Speaks loudly enough to be heard at all times	May be hard to hear part of the time	Mumbles; may be hard to hear most of the time
	Visual aids demonstrate effective use of lettering, layout, and other elements of design	Visual aids show an attempt to incorporate elements of design	Visual aids show poor craftsmanship
	Visual aids contain correct grammar, punctuation, capitalization, and spelling	Visual aids contain some errors in grammar, punctuation, capitalization, and spelling, which may detract slightly from their effectiveness	Visual aids contain so many errors in grammar, punctuation, capitalization, and spelling, that they distract attention from the message

Figure 2.3 Rubric for Oregon Trail

Task

Students take on the persona of a person traveling overland to Oregon or California in the 1840s. They are to write a diary about (at least 15 entries) and make a map of their journey. They should include the following things:

- Where they went. The journey should make sense in terms of where travelers would have gone and the order in which locations would have been visited. All locations should be named as they would have been at the time of the trip.

- Important dates—when they left, when they arrived at various locations, and when they returned.

- Interesting things they encountered—sites or people. These things should represent what travelers really would have encountered.

- Problems they encountered—illnesses, battles, food, water, etc.

Rubric

Criterion	Excellent	Good	Fair	Poor
Originality	The diary and map are very original. The map is colorful and neat. The diary has named characters, and at least 15 entries. The student worked extra hard.	The diary and map are original. The map has colors. The diary has 10 to 15 entries. The student worked hard, but did not expend extra effort.	The story and map are fairly original. There is a map and a diary, but the diary has fewer than 10 entries.	The diary and map are not original. The map is not drawn well and the diary has very few entries.
Readability	Very easy to read. Pictures are glued from the back; the title on the map and diary are neat, titles on the map are large enough to read; the diary is in diary format, with a separate page for each entry.	Readable.	Barely readable.	The diary and/or map are sloppy, dirty, crumpled, or torn. Writing is illegible. There are no titles. The diary is not written in diary format.
Timeliness	All materials completed on time.	Most materials completed on time.	Some materials completed on time.	No materials completed on time.

Weak. Consider the writing rubric in Table 2.2. Chances are, the district, state, or provincial content standards include other features of writing, and experts in the field would agree that this rubric is an incomplete description of writing quality. This rubric is weak because it covers only fluency, articulation, spelling, and completion of the assignment. There *are* other important features of writing. However, if the author stated that the intent is to focus on only a portion of a longer writing rubric, then the content coverage would be less weak.

Indicator B: Criteria are Well Organized

Strong. Refer to the Central Kitsap School District's rubric, *Mathematical Problem Solving: A Three-Trait Model, Adult Version* in Appendix C and on the CD. It is divided into easily understood criteria: *Mathematical Concepts and Procedures, Problem Solving,* and *Mathematical Communication.* The same three traits appear on many other rubrics for assessing the quality of student responses to math problems. The details used to describe a criterion go together. The relative emphasis on criteria is justifiable. The criteria are independent.

Table 2.2 Weak Writing Rubric

4	3	2	1	0
Excellent The writing is fluent and accurate.	Outstanding Good fluency and articulation. Few spelling errors.	Satisfactory Completion, writer exhibits some articulation and fluency.	Not Satisfactory Incomplete, difficult to understand.	Unable to Accomplish the Task

Source: From a rubric presented as a weak example in *Classroom Assignment Scoring Manual, Elementary School* (pp. 27–28) by L. C. Matsumura, J. Pascal, J. R. Steinberg, and R. Valdes, 2002, Los Angeles, CA: CRESST. Copyright ©2002 by the National Center for Research on Evaluation, Standards, and Student Testing (CRESST) and the Regents of the University of California, supported under the Institute of Education Science (IES), U.S. Department of Education. Used with permission.

Medium. Consider the *General Conceptual Understanding Rubric* in Appendix C and on the CD. It has a single criterion, but it seems to cover three distinct criteria: accuracy of knowledge, explanation and support, and communication.

Medium. The rubric *Middle School Oral Presentation* in Table 2.1 is about at the midpoint for quality on the organization of criteria. Descriptors referring to visual aids are present in both criteria, and while they have been divided according to their contribution to *Organization* and *Delivery*, we think this rubric would be easier for students and teachers to use if those descriptors were placed in a separate criterion, such as *Use of Visual Aids*. The descriptor "Is able to answer audience's questions" in *Organization*, although in an oral presentation following logically after the conclusion, does not belong in this criterion. If it is important, it may also need its own category; or it might go in a criterion for *Content Understanding*, should one be added.

Weak. Think about the *Job Application Letter Scoring Guide* in Figure 2.2. The rubric is out of balance, with the format of the letter counting much more than its content. The rubric is a seemingly endless list. As indicated previously, we might solve the problem of too many features to rate by grouping like indicators together into four criteria.

Weak. Consider the *Book Report Rubric* in Table 2.3. Although there are some *Content* issues (*Rubric for Rubrics* indicator 1A)—some of what is on the rubric probably should not be there (such as the formatting statements, if the intended learning targets are in the subject of Reading)—we'll focus on the *Organization* issues (*Rubric for Rubrics* indicator 1B). The content that *is* pertinent to a book report seems mixed up; it would be clearer if it were organized into criteria. You could group characters, setting and plot together; spelling, punctuation, capitalization, and grammar together (subject/verb agreement is generally considered to be a part of grammar); and then pay careful attention to the learning targets the book report is supposed to assess to create a third category having, perhaps, to do with comprehension, interpretation, and/or evaluation of the book.

Indicator C: Number of Levels Fits Targets and Uses

Most rubrics have an appropriate number of levels—3 to 6. You occasionally run across one with problems in this area. We've already seen one rubric where the number of levels would *not* work—the *Job Application Letter Scoring Guide* in Figure 2.2. In this case it is hard to see how many features, such as "has two hard returns after the closing," can be rated on a three-point scale. A checklist (for *present* or *absent*) seems more appropriate.

Another example of scoring scales with too many levels would be the common practice of assigning large numbers of points for various features of the work; for example: "quality of the writing gets 25 points and the use of references gets 10 points." This example has 25 possible levels of quality for writing and 10 for references. It would be difficult to distinguish among the levels.

Activity 2.1

Compare Rubrics on the *Rubric for Rubrics* Criterion of *Coverage/Organization*

In the *Rubric Sampler* on the CD, find rubrics that you think are Strong, Medium, and Weak (if any) on the *Rubric for Rubrics* criterion of *Coverage/Organization*. Justify your judgment using wording from the *Rubric for Rubrics*.

If you are working with others, compare your ratings. Come to a group rating. Justify this rating using language from the *Coverage/Organization* criterion.

Table 2.3 Book Report Rubric

Exceeds Standard (5 points for each)	Meets standard (4 points for each)	Approaches Standard (2 points for each)	Below Standard (0 points for each)
Includes the following information: title of the book, author, copyright, publisher, and date	Includes most of the following information: title of the book, author, copyright, publisher, and date	Includes some of the following information: title of the book, author, copyright, publisher, and date	Missing most or all of the following information: title of the book, author, copyright, publisher, and date
Typed, 12 point Times Roman font; two pages; 1.5 spaced	Typed, 12 point Times Roman font; a page and a half; 1.5 spaced	Not typed; one page	Not typed, less than one page
Meets the requirements of the assignment	Meets most of the requirements of the assignment	Meets some of the requirements of the assignment	Does not meet the requirements of the assignment
Information shared shows insightful understanding of the book	Information shared shows adequate understanding of the book	Information shared shows partial understanding of the book	Information shared does not show understanding of the book
Conclusion clearly states your opinion about the book	Conclusion states your opinion about the book	Conclusion is present, but does not state your opinion about the book	Conclusion is missing
Main characters are thoroughly described	Main characters are described	Some main characters are described	Main characters are not described
Setting is clearly identified	Setting is identified	Setting is incompletely identified	Setting is not identified
Plot is summarized completely	Plot is summarized adequately	Plot is partially summarized	Plot is not summarized
Title page + illustration	Title page + illustration	Title page + illustration	Title page + illustration missing
Timeline includes 10 or more important events	Timeline includes 7–9 important events	Timeline includes 4–6 important events	Timeline includes 3 or fewer important events
All spelling is correct	3–5 spelling mistakes	6–10 spelling mistakes	More than 10 spelling mistakes
All punctuation is correct	1–2 punctuation mistakes	3–5 punctuation mistakes	More than 6 punctuation mistakes
All capitalization is correct	1–2 capitalization mistakes	3–4 capitalization mistakes	More than 5 capitalization mistakes
Correct grammar	1 grammar mistake	2–3 grammar mistakes	More than 3 grammar mistakes
Correct subject/verb agreement	1 subject/verb agreement problem	2 subject/verb agreement problems	3 or more subject/verb agreement problems

Understanding *Rubric for Rubrics* Criterion 2: *Clarity*

Consider the *Rubric for Rubrics* criterion of *Clarity*. Once again, begin by reading the indicators and descriptors for the high level, *5—Strong*. Highlight any words or phrases that jump out at you as particularly indicating a strong performance. Then do the same for the low level, *1—Weak*, and finally for the middle level, *3—Medium*.

Indicator A: Levels Defined

Strong. The classic example of a conscious attempt to maximize clarity is the *6 + 1 Trait™ Writing Assessment Scoring Guide*. The various authors have provided descriptors that enable a person to match the wording in the rubric to the work being examined. Notice that there are no vague comparison words such as *extremely* or *little*; no hint of vague quantities such as "almost always" or "seldom," and no sign of counts such as "no more than one error" or "more than 10 errors." There are also student-friendly versions available (see the CD for one example).

Strong. Read the *Research Paper Rubric* (in Appendix C and on the CD). Consider the fifth bullet on the criterion of *Communication*. Descriptors at the High, Average, and Low levels are, "quotations, paraphrases and summaries are used and cited appropriately," "quotations, paraphrases and summaries generally work but occasionally interfere with the flow of the writing, seem irrelevant, or are incorrectly cited," and "quotations, paraphrases and summaries tend to break the flow of the piece, become monotonous, don't seem to fit, and/or are not cited," respectively. This provides guidance on what contributes to a judgment of *good quotations, paraphrases, or summaries*. Many of the other descriptors likewise give guidance on what makes a component of the research report work or not work.

Medium. Look at the *Seminar Discussion Rubric* (in Appendix C and on the CD). There is descriptive detail, such as, "selects details from the text to support interpretations," and "the student develops understanding of themes, main ideas, and supporting details." But the scoring guide also includes some vague differentiations; for example, the only difference between *excellent* and *proficient* on one descriptor is "the student shows perception while actively developing understanding of themes, main ideas, and supporting details," versus "the student shows thoughtfulness as understanding of themes, main ideas, and supporting details develops." Maybe the teacher can tell the difference between *perceptiveness* and *thoughtfulness*, but can students? Would other teachers interpret the difference similarly? Clarity would be improved by descriptions of *perceptiveness* and *thoughtfulness*.

Medium. Read the *General Science Rubric* (in Appendix C and on the CD). Some descriptive detail appears. For example, the Expert level on the trait of *Scientific Communication* contains "the reader does not need to infer how and why decisions were made" and "interpretation of data . . . raised new questions or was applied to new contexts." But there are also instances of vague comparison words. For example, consider the difference between Expert and Practitioner on the criterion of *Scientific Procedures and Reasoning*: "accurately and proficiently" versus "effectively." What's the difference? What evidence would you look for? The rubric phrases should describe the difference clearly.

Weak. Refer to the Oregon Trail scoring guide in Figure 2.3. Although there is an attempt to define levels, the comparisons are vague. How do we differentiate between "the map is colorful" and "the map has colors," or "worked extra hard" and "worked hard?" Also, the diary is judged on the number of entries. Is it true that quality in the diary is created mainly through the number of entries?

Figure 2.4 Inconsistent Content Across Levels

Scoring Guide for Science Journal	
Novice	Writing is messy and contains spelling errors. Pages are out of order or missing.
Apprentice	Entries are incomplete. There might be some spelling or grammar errors.
Master	Entries contain most of the required elements and are clearly written.
Expert	Entries are creatively written. Procedures and results are clearly explained. Journal is well organized; presented in a duotang.

Source: From "What's Still Wrong with Rubrics: Focusing on the Consistency of Performance Criteria Across Scale Levels," by R. Tierney & M. Simon, 2004, *Practical Assessment, Research & Evaluation, 9*(2), p. 5. Used with permission.

Rubric for Presentations	
Failing	Student does not understand the topic, gives a weak presentation, cannot be heard, uses a diagram unrelated to the topic, and does not look at the audience.
Mediocre	Student has not chosen an important topic, presentation and diagram are weak, and has not tried very hard.
Acceptable	Student has chosen a topic that is OK but is too broad, understands something about the topic, and uses a diagram that is somewhat related to the topic.
Strong	Student has chosen a topic that is difficult, explains this topic well, and understands the topic.
Superior	The student's work is exceptional, has shown a lot of effort, is interesting to listen to, and is creative.

Weak. Look at the *Rubric for Presentations* in Figure 2.4. Although there are other problems with this rubric, we focus here on the judgmental language. Such terms as *mediocre* and *failing* do not help students to perform better next time, and may actually serve to decrease student motivation to try again.

Weak. Look at the *General Understanding Rubric* in Table 2.4. Although it covers some relevant aspects of the task (*Rubric for Rubrics* criterion 1: *Coverage/Organization*), the descriptions of these criteria need more detail. For example, how do the following descriptors under Score Point 4 differ?

- Demonstrates in-depth knowledge about the topic.

- Demonstrates in-depth understanding of the relevant and important ideas.

- Shows a depth of understanding of important relationships.

Additionally, vague words are used to differentiate levels. For example, what is the difference between "demonstrates in-depth knowledge about the topic" at level 4 and "demonstrates knowledge about the topic" at level 3?

Weak. Although the *Book Report Rubric* in Table 2.3 has levels, it would be difficult to distinguish among them in many cases. What is the difference between "Conclusion clearly states your opinion about the book" and "Conclusion states your opinion about the book"? What is the difference between "insightful understanding" and "adequate understanding"? This rubric demonstrates the limitations of using a formula or a computer program to generate a rubric. You just do not get enough descriptive detail to match a student performance to a score with confidence. Also, in the descriptor about the timeline, frequency counts stand in for a description of quality. Does number of events encompass what we look for in a well-executed timeline? We do not think so.

Indicator B: Levels Parallel

Strong. Both the *Technical Writing Rubric* and the Clackamas Community College *Research Paper Rubric* (in Appendix C and on the CD) have levels that are strictly parallel—every feature that appears on one level also appears on every other level.

Table 2.4 General Understanding Rubric

Only two of the four levels are shown because this is enough to discern the type of description in the rubric.

Score Point	Criteria for Scoring
4	• Demonstrates in-depth knowledge about the topic.
	• Demonstrates in-depth understanding of the relevant and important ideas.
	• Includes the important ideas related to the topic and shows a depth of understanding of important relationships.
	• Defines concepts and principles and uses examples and quotations to demonstrate understanding.
	• Developed fully and includes specific facts or examples.
	• Organized somewhat around big ideas, major concepts/principles in the field.
	• Contains no misconceptions.
	• Uses all terms correctly.
	• Demonstrates a logical and coherent plan of organization.
	• The response is exemplary, detailed, and clear.
3	• Demonstrates knowledge about the topic.
	• Demonstrates a good understanding of the topic.
	• Includes some of the important ideas related to the topic.
	• Shows a good understanding of the important relationships.
	• Demonstrates good development of ideas and includes adequate supporting facts or examples.
	• May demonstrate some organization around big ideas, major concepts/principles in the field.
	• The response is good, has some detail, and is clear.

Medium. Although the *Teaming Rubric* (in Appendix C and on the CD) is very strong in most respects, it might do with a little more scrutiny on parallelism. Look at the first criterion, *Collaborative Climate*. Level 5 includes leadership; the other levels do not. The first bullet (performance reviews) and fourth bullet (new ideas) at level 3 are also represented at level 1, but not at level 5. It's possible that "forward-focused evaluation" refers to performance reviews, but it is not clear. Is this a problem? It appears so, but the final word would should come from an expert on teaming. It may be that there are fundamentally different indicators of *Collaborative Climate* at various levels of performance.

Weak. Figure 2.4 shows two rubrics that are seriously inconsistent in content across levels.

In the *Scoring Guide for Science Journal*, the Novice level has descriptors relating to neatness, conventions, and presentation. The Apprentice level has descriptors relating to completeness and conventions. The Master level has descriptors relating to completeness and clarity of writing. The Expert level has descriptors relating to creativity, clarity of writing, organization, and presentation method. Parallelism of levels requires that we describe all characteristics of quality at each level.

For the *Rubric for Presentations*, the Failing level has descriptors relating to knowledge, diagram, and presentation (eye contact and volume); Mediocre has descriptors on topic selected, effort, diagram, and presentation; Acceptable includes the topic chosen, diagram, and knowledge; Strong includes the topic chosen, presentation, and knowledge; and Exceptional includes effort, presentation, and creativity.

Weak. The writing rubric in Table 2.2 also has consistency problems across levels. See if you can spot them.

Exceptions. Consider the *Reading Developmental Continuum* (in Appendix C and on the CD). The levels are parallel in the sense that the same three criteria (comprehension, skills/strategies, and attitudes/behaviors) appear at all levels. The descriptors at each level change to describe what students are doing at a particular level of development. We would say that this is all right because hallmarks of development might be different at each level.

Parallelism is a virtue to be *consciously* abandoned when it doesn't provide the best way to differentiate levels of performance.

For More Practice

Additional rubrics appear in the *Rubric Sampler* on the CD. Each general rubric in the *Sampler* is evaluated using the *Rubric for Rubrics*. These evaluations appear in a separate file on the CD or on the ETS Assessment Training Institute website (http://www.assessmentinst.com/rubrics).

Activity 2.2

Compare Rubrics on the *Rubric for Rubrics* Trait of *Clarity*

In the *Rubric Sampler* on the CD, find classroom rubrics that you think are Strong, Medium, and Weak on the *Rubric for Rubrics* criterion of *Clarity*. Justify your judgment using wording from the *Rubric for Rubrics*.

If you are working in a group, compare your ratings. Come to a group rating. Justify this rating using language from the *Clarity* criterion.

Activity 2.3

Audit a Rubric You Use

1. Choose a rubric from among those you use that you would like to improve.

2. Audit it for quality using the *Rubric for Rubrics*.

3. Revise the rubric based on your conclusions.

Misconception Alert

Anything Goes in a Student-Developed Rubric

While we're all in favor of involving students in rubric development, it is *not* true that anything goes when we do. We have to be ready to lead students to germane criteria. We have to have a clear picture in our own minds of where we want to take students so that we can engage them in activities and show them models that lead them to justified inferences about quality. Teachers generally know more about quality than do students. Even though students always have knowledge to build on, they also can harbor misunderstandings. Our rubrics send a message to students about what is important. Therefore, the rubrics they create have to cover the features that really *do* define a quality performance or product.

We once saw a rubric developed by third graders to evaluate reading comprehension by producing a poster of the story. Students focused on the quality considerations for an attractive poster—three colors, at least five pictures, neat, readable from a distance, and so on—instead of the quality of the *comprehension* displayed by the poster.

A solution? How about leading these students to deliberately evaluate two different criteria: comprehension of the story as revealed by the poster and the attractiveness of the poster itself. For the former, have them think about what would indicate that a student has understood the story. For the latter, let them know that it is always important to present work in an engaging manner. Here their criteria for a quality poster might prove sufficient.

Then, if we put two scores in the record book—comprehension and presentation—it would be clear what each score is evidence of. The presentation score would be used in figuring an art grade, not a reading grade, because the rubric for presentation represents art-related learning targets.

Misconception Alert
The Purpose of Rubrics Is to Help Students Score High

Of course we want rubrics to help students do well. But there is a subtlety here that can cause thinking to go astray. Are we using rubrics to define quality or to help students get a good score on an assignment? Hopefully, it is both. But sometimes when we stress the latter, we neglect the former.

If we want rubrics to only help students get an A, we can include anything we want—answer all five questions, have a colorful cover, include at least three pictures, make it three pages long, write your response as a story, use a five-paragraph organizational pattern, and so on. Students can get an A if they know it takes these things to do so. But, what message does it send students about what is important or what to attend to when producing a quality piece of work? "I get it, a good piece of writing is as least three pages long and uses a five-paragraph organizational pattern."

We're not arguing that students should never have to write, for example, a five-paragraph theme. But you never want to leave the impression that *only* a five-paragraph theme constitutes good writing or that students who have written five paragraphs have demonstrated an element of quality.

Summary

1. Not every rubric is equally useful in the classroom, especially if you want to use your rubric as an instructional tool with students.

2. The *Rubric for Rubrics* is a tool to help decide which rubrics to use in the classroom as instructional tools.

3. The *Rubric for Rubrics* identifies two criteria for quality: *Coverage/Organization* and *Clarity*.

4. The criterion of *Coverage/Organization* focuses on the statements in the classroom rubric about what features of student work will count, how these features are organized into major dimensions (criteria), and the number of levels in the rubric. Plusses include samples of student work and student-friendly versions.

5. The *Rubric for Rubrics* criterion of *Clarity* covers how well the features and levels in the classroom rubric are defined and the degree to which levels are parallel.

6. After scrutinizing hundreds of rubrics and scoring guides, developing rubrics, and helping others develop them, we have noticed several rubric pitfalls that are easy to fall into:

   - Being clear enough for teachers to judge quality but not for students to understand

   - Using a task-specific scoring guide when a general one is better

   - Using a holistic rubric when an analytic one is better

   - Using counts as an indicator of quality when quantity is not equivalent to quality

   - Including criteria that evaluate adherence to directions of the task rather than level of mastery of the target

   - In the interest of usability, trying to shorten a rubric for a complex target so that it fits onto a single page

   - Misreading the real purpose of rubrics: It is to help students learn how to improve, not simply to get a good grade

chapter

$$\left[\ 3\ \right]$$

How to Develop a
General Rubric

*The key assessment question comes down to this: . . .
Do I know the difference between successful and unsuccessful
performance and can I convey that difference in
meaningful terms to my students?*

—R. J. Stiggins
Student-Involved Classroom Assessment (3rd ed),
Upper Saddle River, NJ: Merrill/Prentice Hall, 2001, p. 196

This chapter focuses on developing general rubrics for class-room use.

We recommend begging, borrowing, and stealing (well, maybe not stealing) general rubrics if at all possible. Develop them only if a survey of what is available yields no promising candidates. General analytic rubrics take time to develop well if they are to represent the features of a quality performance or product clearly and accurately. The learning target to be assessed by the rubric has to be worth the time spent. Rubric development is useful when learning targets are

- Fuzzy yet important, and you would like to see clearly what it will look like as students progress toward mastery.

- Those students always seem to have trouble with, and you would like to make them clearer to students.

- Shared across teachers and/or grade levels, and it would be useful to have a common vocabulary for teachers and students when talking about quality.

Rubric Development

The steps in creating a general rubric always involve some combination of collecting samples of existing rubrics, brainstorming features of good performance, examining and scoring student work, and refining. It is useful to do this work with others. Working in a group that includes experts on the targets in question is even more useful.

We discuss two variations on this process. The first and most complex is when you don't really know what criteria, indicators, or descriptors will emerge in your final rubric. The second, simpler version is when you already have a good idea of the criteria to be represented in your rubric.

Developing a Rubric When the Criteria Are Unclear

We describe here an eight-step process, using the *Research Paper Rubric* (found on the CD and in Appendix C) as our running example. Additional development examples can be found for first-year foreign language in Stiggins et al., 2004, Chapter 7; and for writing, mathematics problem solving, and self-reflection in Arter & McTighe, 2001, Chapter 4.

Step 1: Choose a Learning Target Worth the Time

Before you go to the trouble and expense of developing a rubric from scratch, be certain that the learning target you intend to assess is worth the effort. For example, the *Research Paper Rubric* was developed by teachers in several community colleges who were teaching an interdisciplinary freshman inquiry course. The teachers wanted to make sure that student performance in the inquiry class meant the same thing across several campuses.

The umbrella concept for the course was "understand and appreciate how change occurs." The specific course content varied from teacher to teacher, from examining how change occurs in art to how it occurs in science. Students were to write a research paper on some aspect of change—personal change or changes in culture or ideas. Therefore, the instructors wanted a rubric for the paper general enough to cover whatever focus students chose.

Step 2: Search out Existing Relevant Scoring Guides

It is important to collect available existing rubrics and descriptions of expert performance. These documents can provide you with both inspiration and actual rubric language. The community college teachers in our example were able to find sample rubrics for potential criteria of a research paper. (Two of these appear in the *Rubric Sampler* on the CD and in

Appendix C: the *6 + 1 Trait™ Writing Assessment Scoring Guide* and the *General Conceptual Understanding* rubric. Other sources for rubrics are in the CD file, *Performance Assessment Resources.*)

Step 3: Gather Samples of Student Work

Gather samples of student work (from your previous courses, or from colleagues, books, or the Internet) that you feel represent the broadest range of student performance on the learning target(s) to be assessed. In general, try to have at least 20 samples representing more than one topic or task. Using samples from only one topic or task might lead you to develop what amounts to a task-specific rubric, one that can only be used to judge the quality of the performance or product created for a single assignment. A variety of samples helps ensure that all important general criteria end up on the final rubric.

Step 4: Sort Student Work

A good place to begin is by examining the samples of student work and sorting them into three stacks, representing your evaluation of them as strong, medium, and weak (or proficient, developing, and beginning, or whatever other terms make sense in your setting), and writing down your reasons as you go. If you are fortunate enough to be part of a development team, have each member do this independently and then determine the consensus. Here is the important part: *The goal of sorting is not necessarily to get every sample in exactly the correct stack. The goal is to develop as long a list as possible of the reasons why you place each sample in its respective stack.* Eventually, of course, you want to be able to judge samples accurately and consistently, but that is not the goal now.

Be as descriptive as possible with your reasons—this will jumpstart the descriptive detail you will want in your final rubric. Here are two ways we have found to create descriptive detail:

1. For each sample, write down exactly what you are saying to yourself as you place it into a stack. Don't wait until you have the samples sorted. It is harder to remember later all the details of your reasons.

2. Jot down comments you would make to provide feedback to the student on what was done well and how to make the performance or product better next time.

Following are examples of phrases with descriptive detail:

- I'm confused—I can't follow the reasoning.
- The ideas are mixed up; ideas that go together aren't placed together.
- The topic chosen is focused. It is of the size that it can be discussed well in the context of this paper.
- The important ideas are identified. The important information has been selected for use.
- The student has not taken a position on the issue.
- Calculations are accurate at the beginning but not at the end.
- The solution shows evidence that the student has checked her answer for reasonableness.

These descriptive statements will form the core of your rubric descriptors. Avoid broad statements such as "the solution is logical," "the writing has appropriate voice," or "not well organized" for two reasons. First, although teachers might understand these statements, students probably will not. Second, such broad statements as "it's logical" are based on a variety of specific characteristics in the work. What you want to generate is a list of those characteristics you base your judgment on, so that students will know what *logical* means.

Dig below general statements when possible. Exactly what in the work leads to your conclusion that the solution is logical, the voice is good, or that the piece is not well organized? For example, indicators for *logical* might be that no steps are left out, the steps are in the right order, no unneeded steps are included, the process is easy to follow, and no inferences are required.

As another example, aspects of the work that indicate to you that the work is *not well organized* might be that ideas that go together are not placed together, the paper jumps around from topic to topic with few guiding transitions, there is no opening information to tell the reader where the paper is going, and there is no conclusion—the paper just stops.

There will always be some degree of ambiguity; that's in the nature of a general rubric. The goal is to reduce this ambiguity as much as possible by being as descriptive as possible. (The other way to reduce ambiguity is to choose illustrative samples for each level, as we will describe in Step 6 and discuss in more detail in Chapter 6.)

Table 3.1 shows the community college teachers' list of brainstormed descriptors. Note that the middle level shows a balance of strengths and weaknesses—some of this, but also a lack of that. Note also that this initial list contains a mix of descriptive detail and broad statements such as *sound analysis* and *logical.*

As people sort samples, they frequently ask if they can create more than three levels, feeling that three is too few. Their eye develops to the point that they find work that is between two of the levels and they want to have four to six stacks. This is the beginning of determining your final number of levels. If three seems adequate, that's your number. If people can easily distinguish more levels, in fact, *want* more levels, then you'll probably end up with more.

Table 3.1 Brainstormed List of Descriptors for a Research Paper

Strong	Facts are accurate; topic of the paper addresses change; author has a good grasp of what is known, what is generally accepted, and what is yet to be discovered; introduction draws the reader in; spelling is correct; terminology is used correctly; citations use the proper format; quotations support the author's points; transitions are thoughtful and clearly show how ideas connect; punctuation is accurate; an appropriate balance of factual reporting, interpretation, analysis, and personal opinion; details support the author's arguments; irrelevant information is rarely included; connections between the topic of the paper and related topics are made that enhance understanding; the conclusion is satisfying, leaving the reader with a sense of closure; reader is convinced; reader is left with few questions; punctuation is correct; sequencing is logical and effective; punctuation and grammar add flair; sound analysis; logical.
Middle	Recognizable introduction, but it doesn't create a strong sense of anticipation; spelling generally correct, but sometimes distracting; paper is almost complete, but leaves out at least one important aspect of the problem; balance between facts, interpretation, and personal opinion is skewed; facts are generally accurate; the conclusion is there, but it doesn't tie the paper together; some ideas are obvious or elementary; sometimes uses information inappropriate to its significance; some irrelevant information is included; terminology is sometimes used correctly and sometimes not; some connections between ideas are fuzzy; sources generally support the author's points, but there are too few cited; quotes generally work, but sometimes interfere with the flow; some words are misspelled; incorrect grammar sometimes gets in the way of clarity; the reader is left with a few questions; sequencing mostly works, but sometimes is confusing; some connections between ideas fuzzy.
Weak	No lead in to set up what follows; most ideas seem obvious or elementary; the topic of the paper needs to be more about change; many relevant issues left out; no connections made to related topics to help clarify the information presented; terminology frequently misused; paper seems a simple restatement of the assignment; paper reads like a brainstormed list of ideas; no discernable conclusion; citations are infrequent; citations don't seem to support the author's points; spelling, punctuation, and grammar problems get in the way of understanding the author's points; connections between ideas are confusing; quotations get in the way of the flow; spelling and punctuation errors are distracting; frequent spelling errors even on common words; analysis superficial; little understanding of the relevant issues; ideas that go together are not together; quotations are monotonous; few details support the author's argument; the reader is unconvinced.

Variation on the Theme
Four Preset Levels

In some settings you will be developing rubrics with four preset levels: exceeds the standard, meets the standard, approaches the standard, and doesn't meet the standard. In this case, begin with two stacks—clearly meets the standard and clearly doesn't meet the standard. Put work you are not sure of in a separate pile. Later you can divide the clearly meets the standard stack into exceeds and meets, and the clearly doesn't meet the standard into approaches and not close piles. As your eye gets better at noticing subtle distinctions, you can begin to place and describe the ambiguous samples.

Step 5: Group Like Indicators Together

As people brainstorm, they often become increasingly uncomfortable with placing work along a single continuum of quality because individual examples are frequently stronger in some ways and weaker in others. For example, "the use of quotations is excellent, but there are quite a few spelling errors," or "the points made are good, but the organization could be better." This is the beginning of the analytical structure for the rubric. When people can sort out broad categories of relative strength or weakness, these indicate separate criteria clusters.

It is also frequently the case that many descriptors on the original brainstormed list of key attributes are closely linked and can be grouped together. Where you note distinct categories, you have created an initial list of separate criteria. At this stage refining criteria takes place; you might decide that two criteria really refer to the same thing, or that one criterion should be divided into two or more criteria because of their independent importance. Most rubrics go through several stages of criteria definition and organization.

For the *Research Paper Rubric*, the teachers noted that three broad criteria categories seemed to emerge: *Communication* (writing), *Critical Thinking*, and *Content Understanding*. They proceeded by attempting to sort all the descriptors into these three groups, ending with the draft rubric shown in Table 3.2. This draft is essentially the descriptors from the brainstormed list sorted into categories. Note that some language is borrowed from the *6 + 1 Trait™ Writing Assessment Scoring Guide* (beg, borrow, and steal!). The teachers also decided that the *Critical Thinking* and *Content* criteria were more important than the *Communication* criterion and doubled the number of points possible for them.

Variation on the Theme
Six Levels

Sometimes people decide to use six levels, where level 6 is *the best I've ever seen*. This is done because sometimes when using five levels, level 5 becomes *the best I've ever seen*, thus reducing the effective number of levels to four. The sixth level is added to make it easy to use all of what is in practice a five-level rubric.

Table 3.2 First Draft of the Research Paper Rubric

Communication Score (circle one): I 2 3 4 5		
High Mastery	*Average Mastery*	*Low Mastery*
5 points: an inviting introduction draws the reader in, a satisfying conclusion leaves the reader with a sense of closure and resolution; transitions are thoughtful and clearly show how ideas connect; sources are well integrated and support the author's points; effective use of summary, paraphrase, and quotation; uses the proper format (APA, MLA, etc.); sequencing is logical and effective; spelling is generally correct, even on more difficult words; punctuation is accurate, even creative, and guides the reader effectively through the text; grammar and usage contribute to the clarity; conventions, if manipulated for stylistic effect, work; the piece is very close to being ready to publish.	**3 points:** the paper has a recognizable introduction and conclusion, but the introduction may not create a strong sense of anticipation and/or the conclusion may not tie the paper into a coherent whole; transitions often work well, but some leave connections between ideas fuzzy; sources generally support the author's points but there are too few cited; quotes and paraphrases generally work but occasionally interfere with the flow of the writing or seem irrelevant; uses the proper format but there are occasional errors; sequencing shows some logic but it is not under complete control and may be so predictable that the reader finds it distracting; spelling is generally correct but more difficult words may be misspelled; end punctuation is correct but internal punctuation is sometimes missing or wrong; there are problems with grammar or usage but not serious enough to distort meaning; the piece needs moderate amount of editing to be ready to publish.	**I point:** there is no real lead-in to set up what follows, no real conclusion to wrap things up; connections between ideas are often confusing or missing; citations are infrequent or often seem to fail to support the author's points; quotations and paraphrases break the flow of the piece, become monotonous, or don't seem to fit with the point the author is making; frequent errors in format or incorrect format used; sequencing seems illogical, disjointed, or forced; there are frequent spelling errors even on common words, punctuation is often missing or incorrect, including terminal punctuation; errors in grammar or usage are frequent enough to become distracting and interfere with meaning; extensive editing would be required to prepare the text for publication.

Table 3.2 (Continued)

Content Understanding Score (circle one): 1 2 3 4 5		
High Mastery	*Average Mastery*	*Low Mastery*
10 points: the paper addresses a topic within the context of promoting personal, social/cultural/ political, or paradigmatic change; the paper is complete and leaves no important aspect of the topic unaddressed; the author has a good grasp of what is known, what is generally accepted, and what is yet to be discovered; appropriate significance is assigned to the information presented; irrelevant information is rarely included; connections between the topic of the paper and related topics are made that enhance understanding; specialized terminology, if used, is used correctly and precisely; the author seems to be writing from personal knowledge or experience.	**6 points:** the paper addresses a topic within the context of promoting personal, social/cultural/ political, or paradigmatic change; the paper is substantially complete but more than one important aspect of the topic is unaddressed; the author has a good grasp of the relevant information, but fails to distinguish between what is known, what is generally accepted, and what is yet to be discovered; the paper often uses information in a way inappropriate to its significance or includes much irrelevant information; there are few connections made to related topics; specialized terminology is sometimes incorrectly or imprecisely used; the author seems to be writing from knowledge or experience but has difficulty going from general observations to specifics.	**2 points:** the topic of the paper needs to be substantially more closely related to promoting personal, social/cultural/political, or paradigmatic change; the paper is clearly incomplete with many important aspects of the topic left out; the author has a poor grasp of the relevant information; the paper frequently uses information inappropriately or uses irrelevant information; no connections are made to related topics to help clarify the information presented; specialized terminology is frequently misused; the work seems to be a simple restatement of the assignment or a simple, overly broad answer to a question with little evidence of expertise on the part of the author.

Table 3.2 (Continued)

Critical Thinking Score (circle one): 1 2 3 4 5		
High Mastery	*Average Mastery*	*Low Mastery*
10 points: the paper displays insight and originality of thought; there is sound and logical analysis that reveals clear understanding of the relevant issues; there is an appropriate balance of factual reporting, interpretations and analysis, and personal opinion; the author goes beyond the obvious in constructing interpretation of the facts; telling and accurate details are used to reinforce the author's arguments; the paper is convincing and satisfying.	**6 points:** there are some original ideas, but many seem obvious or elementary; analysis is generally sound, but there are lapses in logic or understanding; paper shows understanding of relevant issues, but lacks depth; the balance between factual reporting, interpretation and analysis, and personal opinion seems skewed; generally accurate details are included but the reader is left with questions—more information is needed to 'fill in the blanks'; the paper leaves the reader vaguely skeptical and unsatisfied.	**2 points:** there are few original ideas, most seem obvious or elementary; analysis is superficial or illogical; the author seems to struggle to understand the relevant issues; there is a clear imbalance between factual reporting, interpretation and analysis, and personal opinion; there are few details or most details seem irrelevant; the paper leaves the reader completely unconvinced.

Source: Copyright ©2002, Dave Arter, Clackamas Community College, Oregon City, OR. Adapted with permission.

Step 6: Identify Student Work That Illustrates Each Level on Each Criterion

Following are rules of thumb for selecting student samples to illustrate criteria and levels:

1. *Start with the extremes.* Identify what you consider to be classic examples of strong and weak performances or products—ones that match a good number of the descriptors in the highest and lowest categories. Choose samples that everyone can agree on. When teachers (and students) first begin this analysis, they need examples that are easy to distinguish. Leave more ambiguous examples until later, when users have developed their eye for quality.

Creating & Recognizing Quality Rubrics

2. *Find examples for the middle if you are using an odd number of levels.* The middle is a balance of strengths and weaknesses—the sample displays some of the good characteristics, but also some of the problems.

3. *Find several different examples that illustrate each level. Find examples across assignments.* You don't want your rubric to communicate that there is only a single way to create a strong oral presentation, essay, or experiment. (Because reasoning proficiencies, performance skills, and products are complex learning targets, many different examples can usually satisfy the criteria for strong work.) Your rubric needs to represent the range so that (1) not all student work will look alike, and (2) students can begin to generalize—to apply what they learned from one assignment to the next similar assignment.

4. *Keep your eye out for particular examples of the errors your students commonly make.* What does it look like when quotations get in the way of flow, when a music passage is played without feeling, or when an introduction fails to draw the reader in?

For the *Research Paper Rubric*, the teachers selected samples to illustrate various specific problems and degrees of mastery they found to be common to papers across all their subjects.

The process of finding examples of products or performances usually also results in tweaking the descriptors and criteria of the draft rubric.

Step 7: Test the Rubric and Revise It as Needed

Now it is time to test the rubric in your local situation and note how it could be improved. In Chapter 6, we compile a list of seven strategies that lay out what you can do in the classroom to incorporate assessment *for* learning into daily teaching activities. Use the rubric in these ways with students. Also, score, score, score student samples, and ask students to score some as well! Unless you're spectacularly good at rubric development (or spectacularly lucky), you'll uncover some combination of the following problems:

1. Some student performances or products don't match to descriptors in the rubric. In this case, add descriptors and, perhaps, indicators. Especially try to add descriptors that clarify general features or concepts. Rubrics tend to get larger with all the extra detail. Don't despair; that's part of the revision process. As you continue, you'll begin to pare your rubric down to the truly telling details that seem to cover well the vast majority of what you see in student work.

   This happened with the *Research Paper Rubric*. Between the first draft (Table 3.1) and the current rubric (in Appendix C) three descriptors were added to the criterion of *Communication*: there is a clear thesis; voice and style are appropriate for the type of paper; and paragraphs are well-focused and coherent.

2. Features of student work seem to be rated in more than one criterion. Note these. It might be that some descriptors are redundant across criteria. You need to decide in which criterion a certain feature fits best, or whether to merge criteria to minimize overlap.

3. Criteria should be subdivided, as they seem to cover too much ground or include too many important indicators.

4. The internal structure of the descriptors needs to be improved. This also happened with the *Research Paper Rubric*. The long lists were confusing, and it was hard to compare the descriptors across levels. Notice that on the current version (in Appendix C) descriptors across levels are lined up.

5. The content of some levels is not parallel. You find that some descriptors at one level need counterparts written for the other levels.

As another example, to help us revise the *Rubric for Rubrics* (see Appendix A), we scored about 30 classroom rubrics we had never evaluated before. This process revealed needed revisions in each of the five listed areas. With all our experience with rubrics, there was no substitute for scoring a variety of examples to provide insights on how to improve the *Rubric for Rubrics*.

For the Connoisseur
Use of Samples in Large-Scale Assessment

When using rubrics in the classroom, you generally want samples of student work from across assignments and tasks because your goal is to help students generalize from one task to the next. Your purpose is different when choosing samples for rubrics for large-scale assessments. Here your goal is to judge accurately the particular task to be scored. Therefore, all papers chosen to model levels of quality usually come from that single task.

Step 8: Repeat the Cycle of Scoring and Revising

Rubrics are always works in progress. As you refine your understanding of the learning target through use of the rubric, the rubric becomes more and more precise, comprehensive, and useful. The *Research Paper Rubric* was two years in the making. Is it perfect now? No. Some descriptors are still a little unclear. The indicators in the *Communication* criterion might be organized better, putting the phrases for organization, voice, word choice, sentence fluency, and conventions together.

Does all this take time and effort? You bet. That's why you choose to develop general rubrics only for the most important or least clear learning targets. Is rubric development worth the effort? Absolutely. If you hang in there, this process is guaranteed to clarify fuzziness and result in a scoring guide that can be used across teachers, assignments, and time. It can also result in a powerful learning tool for students.

Developing a Rubric When You Already Have an Idea of the Structure of the Criteria

Usually these days, educators begin rubric development with an idea of the criteria and/or indicators that need to be included on the rubric. These come from content standards, other rubrics, and the professional literature. The general development steps discussed previously hold when you already have an idea of the content of the rubric, but some steps can be condensed. For example, you might not have to sort and annotate as much student work at the beginning to get an idea of the structure of criteria, or revise the rubric as many times to obtain a usable organization.

For the community college *Research Paper Rubric*, the teachers actually did not begin as much from scratch as we let on. The learning targets for the course were *critical thinking* and *written communication*. The instructors were very unsure, however, about how these targets would play out across subject areas. They reviewed many sample rubrics for writing, critical thinking, and conceptual understanding. After the first two-hour meeting, they had decided on general criteria. One person came up with a draft and they all tried it out. This process repeated three times before they had a product they felt they could use consistently.

As another example, we once assisted a district in developing a rubric for mathematics problem solving. They were familiar with the National Council of Teachers of Mathematics (NCTM) standards and their state and district content standards for math problem solving, which aligned with the NCTM standards. We showed them a half dozen other rubrics, and they had their first draft after a single meeting. A little sorting of student work at the beginning helped everyone see where the features on the other rubrics came from. Additionally, after the draft was developed, they still needed to score, score, score to refine the criteria and descriptors.

As with the *Research Paper Rubric*, your development process can be shortened for many learning targets and content areas, but there are still some targets for which there are no existing rubrics or for which rubrics are completely unsatisfactory. In these cases, you will need to develop a rubric from scratch, using the steps discussed in the previous section.

Activity 3.1

Apply These Ideas to a Rubric You Are Interested in Developing

Identify a learning target for which you wish to develop a rubric. How might you proceed?

First, determine whether you know the criteria or will need to develop a rubric from scratch. If the latter, note how you might apply the eight steps discussed in this chapter to your chosen learning target. Then follow each step in detail until you are satisfied with your result.

Developing Student-Friendly Versions

In Appendix C (and on the *Rubric Sampler* on the CD) we have included student-friendly versions of three rubrics: the *6 + 1 Trait™ Analytic Writing Assessment Scoring Guide*, Central Kitsap District's *Mathematics Problem Solving—A Three-Trait Model*, and the *General Science Rubric* (the student-friendly version of which is titled *Exemplars Primary Science Rubric*). Although you can find many good rubrics these days, good student-friendly versions are rare. You can use the following steps to produce student-friendly versions of your rubrics:

1. Find or develop the adult version of the rubric.

2. Identify the words and phrases in the adult version that you think students in your context might not understand.

3. Look these words up in the dictionary or in textbooks. Sometimes the definition of one word requires looking up other words.

4. Convert the definitions into wording students can understand. Sometimes you need to convert words into one or more sentences.

5. Phrase the student-friendly version in the first person.

6. Try the rubric out with students. Ask for their feedback. Revise as needed.

Examples are shown in Tables 3.3 and 3.4.

Table 3.3 Student-Friendly Language Example 1—Research Paper

Rubric	Research Paper Rubric
Trait	Communication
Descriptor	There is a clear thesis
Word or phrase to be defined	Thesis
Dictionary definition	A statement put forward to be supported or proved.
Student-friendly language	I have told the reader the idea that I want to prove in this report.

Table 3.4 Student-Friendly Language Example 2—Music Composition

Rubric	Rubric for Music Composition
Trait	Organization of Musical Ideas
Descriptor	Uses repetition to establish form
Word(s) or phrase(s) to be defined	Repetition, form
Dictionary definition(s)	Repetition: The repeating of a note or notes. Form: The arrangement of notes to create a pleasing whole.
Student-friendly language	Sometimes I repeat notes, groups of notes, or whole sections of music on purpose to create a pleasing whole.

Activity 3.2

Create a Student-Friendly Version of a Rubric

Follow the steps listed previously to create a student-friendly version of a rubric that you want your students to understand and use.

Summary

1. This chapter focuses on developing general rubrics for classroom use.

2. The first step in developing a rubric is to choose a reasoning, performance skill, or product learning target that is important, and/or is unclear, and/or that students have trouble with, and/or for which it would be useful to use the

same vocabulary across teachers and assignments. Keep it as simple as possible. Choose those targets that could most benefit from having a rubric. Prioritize. Don't try to develop all rubrics you might need at once.

3. Educators seldom need to begin from scratch when developing a rubric. Many available examples are at least good enough to provide ideas about descriptors and criteria. We advocate begging and borrowing from existing sources.

4. Collect at least 20 samples of student performances or products representing various levels of proficiency on the learning target of interest.

5. The rest of the development steps depend on how much you know at the beginning about the organization of your rubric. If you already have a pretty good idea, some of the following steps can be condensed.

   • Sort student samples into three stacks, of differing quality.

   • While sorting, describe your reasons for judging samples as you do.

   • Group these reasons into categories—these become your criteria.

   • Develop a draft rubric by grouping like indicators together under their appropriate criteria.

   • Select examples of student performances or products to illustrate all quality levels on each criterion.

   • Try the rubric out and revise it as needed.

6. Students will not always understand the wording of the rubric, even when teachers do. For classroom use it is a good idea to identify the words, phrases, and ideas students might have trouble with, define them, and rewrite the rubric in student-friendly language.

chapter

$$[\ 4\ ]$$

Quality
Performance Tasks

Avoid "products or performances that don't relate to the content" of what is being assessed, even though they may seem like good activities on their own. "Sometimes students get so caught up in the product that they lose sight of what they're actually intending to show with the product."

—J. McTighe
as quoted in "Designing Performance Assessment Tasks,"
Education Update, 37(6), 1995, p. 5

A *performance task* can be thought of as all the material you prepare to let students know what they are supposed to do to demonstrate achievement. It can take one of several forms, depending on the learning target it is intended to assess—a physical demonstration of skill, a verbal presentation or dialogue, or the creation of a product.

We include this chapter on performance tasks because without a good task in place, you won't get an accurate picture of student achievement no matter which rubrics you use. And although the *Rubric for Rubrics* doesn't speak directly to task quality, a task that doesn't give you the performance or product you are looking for will cause problems when you try to use your rubric to evaluate it.

Chances are, you have had experience with a poorly designed task, either on the giving or receiving end. Here are just a few things we know can happen with a poor task:

- Student work doesn't provide evidence of the intended achievement, even if the work is of high quality.

- Students don't know what they are to do and as a result, either don't produce what you expect or don't produce the level of quality they could have had they been clear on what was expected.

- You spend a great deal of time explaining over and over what you want while they are working on the task.

- The task takes much longer to complete than expected.

- The resources necessary for completion turn out to be hard to acquire for some or all students.

- Students find it necessary to get outside help doing the work and/or more of the work than intended has been done by well-meaning parents or other helpers.

- Judging the work turns out to be a nightmare because of all of the achievement targets the task was intended to assess.

These and other problems either compromise the accuracy of the results or waste time, or both. How do we make sure our tasks give us accurate results as efficiently as possible?

Planning for Task Quality

A good task does three things: (1) It elicits the right performance so that you can truly assess what you want to assess. (2) It provides enough evidence to support the uses you intend to make of the information. (3) It avoids the various sources of task bias that can compromise the accuracy of results.

We have developed a rubric for evaluating the quality of a performance task that addresses these three aspects of quality. (This rubric appears in Appendix D.) Remember, however, that before creating or evaluating a task, you need to have established in advance the purpose for the assessment and the intended learning targets to be assessed.

Determining the Purpose of the Assessment

Several decisions, such as what kind of sample you will need, derive directly from the purpose for the assessment. Without this information, you can't determine whether a task is of high quality. You identify the purpose for any assessment by answering three questions:

1. How do I want to use the evidence generated by the task?

2. Who else will use that evidence?

3. How will they use it?

To answer these questions, determine if the task is going to be used as an assessment *of* learning, an assessment *for* learning, or both. Tasks can be considered assessments *of* learning when you intend to use the results to evaluate achievement for reporting purposes—to generate a mark or grade to be included in a final grade, or for accountability purposes—to communicate level of achievement. Tasks that students place in a portfolio to demonstrate their level of achievement or mastery of a set of learning targets are also assessments *of* learning.

Tasks become assessments *for* learning when you use the results before teaching to figure out what students need or to determine how to group students; or part way through the learning to determine what your students have mastered and what you need to reteach, or to group students. In assessment *for* learning contexts, students may also be using the information to determine what they have learned and what they still need to focus on. (We discuss this in more detail in Chapter 6.)

Identifying the Learning Targets to Be Assessed

To identify the learning target or targets you want to assess, write a statement of the intended learning that includes a verb. In many cases, you will be able to find these statements in your district's curriculum guide. Then determine the kind of learning target it is: knowledge, reasoning, performance skill, or product. (For help with this, see Stiggins et al., 2004, Chapter 3.) As stated earlier, performance assessment is a viable option for assessing proficiency with certain patterns of reasoning, performance skill attainment, and the ability to create quality products. Check to make sure that the learning target you intend to assess with a performance assessment is one of these

A note about the importance of identifying the learning target(s): The goal of a performance assessment is to provide evidence of learning. Therefore, before choosing or developing a task it is imperative that you are clear about the learning targets you are teaching. One of the most common problems we see in performance tasks is failure to match the task to the intended learning target. You can anticipate the problem that arises when it comes time to evaluate student work: exactly what do you have evidence of? As you will see, features other than match to target are important, but none are *more* important than that match.

Once you have clearly identified both the purpose for the assessment and the target(s) to be assessed, you are ready to create a high-quality task or to evaluate one for quality.

Criteria for Good Tasks

The rubric we have developed to judge the quality of performance tasks is organized into three categories, or criteria, each with its own set of descriptors (Figure 4.1; see also Appendix D). As you will recall, the *Rubric for Rubrics* (see Appendix A) has an intermediary level of organization—the two criteria are further categorized into indicators and each indicator is followed by one or more descriptors. Because the criteria on the *Rubric for Tasks* do not require subdivisions, it has no indicators.

- Criterion 1: *Content of the Task*—What information does the task need to supply to students?

- Criterion 2: *Sampling*—Is there enough evidence to support the intended purpose?

- Criterion 3: *Distortion Due to Bias*—What can interfere with an accurate picture of student achievement?

Each criterion contains one or more descriptors at each of three levels—Strong, Medium, and Weak.

Task Quality Criterion 1: *Content of the Task*

This criterion lays out what needs to be in the task itself for students to be able to create the performance or product you want.

The first descriptor from the rubric (Appendix D) is as follows (all descriptors given here are from the Strong level unless noted otherwise):

> *All requirements of the task are directly related to the learning target(s) to be assessed. The task will elicit a performance that could be used to judge proficiency on the intended learning targets.*

Figure 4.1 Rubric for Tasks

Content of the Task—What information do students need?

- Requirements of task relate directly to learning target(s).
- Task specifies knowledge to use, performance or product to create, materials to use, timeline.
- Performance skill tasks specify conditions.
- Task specifies help allowed.
- Task includes description of criteria.
- Task provides guidance without over-scaffolding.

Sampling—Is there enough evidence?

- Number of tasks or performances is sufficient for purpose and target.

Distortion Due to Bias—What can interfere with accuracy?

- Instructions are clear.
- Task is narrow enough to be completed in time allotted.
- If choice is offered, options are equivalent.
- Necessary resources are available to all.
- Success does not depend on unrelated skills.
- Success does not depend on cultural experience or language.

Read through your task and ask yourself if it includes any requirement unrelated to the learning target or targets you want to assess.

- Does it ask students to do something that would not provide evidence of their level of achievement on that target? Does it focus on work (or require extra work) that is not needed to measure the intended learning target?

- Does it ask students to do something that provides achievement evidence for a target other than the one you want to assess? Will the performance or product students create demonstrate their level of achievement on your identified learning target(s), or will you get something unrelated that you can't assess with your chosen scoring guide?

If the task scores well on this first descriptor, you are ready to move on. If it doesn't, there is no sense in proceeding. If you scored it as "Medium," you may want to revise it. If you scored it as "Weak," it is off target altogether and you may want to find another task.

The second descriptor on the rubric refers to the actual structure of the task.

The task specifies the following:

- *The knowledge students are to use in its creation*
- *The performance or product students are to create—what form it should take*
- *The materials to be used, if any*
- *Timeline for completion*

Tasks that give students only partial content information cause teachers to spend an inordinate amount of time filling in the missing pieces. *We cannot overstate the importance of avoiding this problem.* Some students, when faced with incomplete information, conclude that because they don't understand what to do, the problem is with them, not with the task. For the duration of that assignment, these students don't regain a sense of confidence that they can be successful. Such tasks are not fair measures of achievement, positive experiences for students, or efficient uses of teacher time.

To understand the parts of this descriptor, let's look at an example.

*Using a stopwatch and a measuring tape, you are
to use your knowledge of the physics of motion to
determine the percentage of vehicles that exceed
the speed limit as they pass the school. Then you
are to write a report in which you explain your
experimental design and share your results.
(Stiggins et al., 2004, p. 222)*

The knowledge to use: Knowledge of the physics of motion

The performance or product: Design an experiment to
determine the percentage of vehicles that exceed the speed
limit. . . . Write a report explaining your design and sharing
your results.

Materials to be used: Stopwatch and measuring tape

Timeline for completion: Missing, but would be easy to add

We begin with a statement of the knowledge to be applied to
remind students of which part of all that we have been studying
they are to focus on. It might appear that this could go without
saying, but many students are thinking about a number of different things besides our course at any given time, and it is only
fair to give them at least a general reminder of the knowledge
they will need to complete the task.

Most tasks include some version of describing the performance or product, but the description may not include enough
details. This particular task has three parts: design an experiment, conduct the experiment, and write a report. Note that
in the third part, "write a report," students are told that their
report must *explain* their experimental design and *share* their
results. Any time you ask students to prepare a written product,
you will get a better-quality product if you specify clearly the
topic (in this case *experimental design* and *results*) and use a
verb to direct them to the kind of writing they are to produce.
What if our task, instead of saying, "Write a report in which you
explain your experimental design and share your results," had

said, "Summarize your results in a report"? Students' reports would not have included evidence of experimental design. Also, the verb *summarize* calls for a much shorter explanation than does *share your results*. In the former case, students could prepare a one-sentence summary and may be at a loss as to how to turn it into a report. Verbs count here. Examine the verbs in a task carefully to make sure they will elicit the desired product or performance.

Including the materials to be used is just common sense. It is better to include this information in the written task rather than relying on students to guess or to remember what you said. However, if part of what is being assessed is knowledge of the ingredients (materials) to be used, then don't list them in the task.

Even though the timeline for completion is not included in this task, again, it is a good idea to let students know in writing how much time they will have to complete the task. Putting it in writing also helps you rethink whether the timeline is reasonable.

Figure 4.2 Ingredients Specific to a Writing Task

- Context
- Format
- Purpose
- Audience
- Topic

Variation on the Theme
Recommendations for the Content of a Writing Task

In certain writing tasks, students benefit from a more in-depth explanation of the knowledge they are to apply and the product they are to create. The following paragraphs discuss specific recommended ingredients for extended writing tasks (see Figure 4.2).

Context. First, give students a context for their writing. The *context* is akin to the knowledge they are to use—it sets the stage for the writing. This is where you can introduce authenticity to the task; that is, choose a context that exemplifies an application of their learning beyond the school context.

Format. If the form the writing will take is not up to the student, the task should identify it—essay, report, magazine article, editorial, poster, play, and so on.

Purpose. In life beyond school, writers generally have a purpose for their writing—to inform, to persuade, to tell a story, and so on. Students also need to know the purpose for their writing—for example, are they to narrate an event, describe something, define something, explain something, judge something, or persuade someone of something? The writing task should include a verb or phrase that clearly points the way to the purpose—for example, *tell the story of, describe/ paint a picture with words, teach, explain, inform*, or *convince*.

Audience. Decisions about content, organization, and style are shaped in part by consideration of the intended audience; a writing task that specifies an audience helps students make these decisions. In life beyond school, who would be reading about this topic?

Topic. Writing tasks don't generally omit the topic, but it may not be stated clearly. What is the writing to be about? Is the topic narrow enough for the time given? Are students to narrow the topic, if necessary?

The third descriptor for *Content of the Task* refers to performance skill tasks:

Tasks assessing a performance skill specify the conditions under which the performance or demonstration is to take place.

Examples of performance skills include giving an oral presentation, reading aloud with fluency, using a table saw safely, conversing in a second language, and playing a musical instrument. A performance skill must be seen or heard to be assessed. For these learning targets, in addition to including the elements described previously, it is helpful to include a description of the conditions such as time limit and context. For example, in assessing the ability to give an oral presentation, will there be a time limit? To whom will the student give the oral presentation?

The fourth descriptor for *Content of the Task* asks us to specify who is allowed to do which parts of the work:

Multi-day tasks specify the help allowed.

Accuracy of results requires that we assess each *student's* achievement, and no one else's. For tasks accomplished in one day, in class, you can control who does the work and what parts students get help with. When work on the task will continue beyond one day, if you don't specify what help is allowed, some students may have a great deal of parent help while others have none. If you want to increase the odds that the work is the student's, the task should explicitly state that as a requirement. On the other hand, for example, if the task requires a written product and you don't intend to evaluate it for spelling, capitalization, or punctuation, you could recommend that students employ a peer or parent editor to help with that part.

The fifth descriptor specifies that you include a reminder of the elements of quality you will use to evaluate the task:

*The task includes a description of the criteria by
which the performance or product will be judged.*

The full text of our previous task example is this:

*Using a stopwatch and a measuring tape, you are
to use your knowledge of the physics of motion to
determine the percentage of vehicles that exceed
the speed limit as they pass the school. Then you
are to write a report in which you explain your
experimental design and share your results. Your
report will be scored on experimental design,
understanding of physics equations, and collection
and presentation of results. Rubrics are attached.
(Stiggins et al., 2004, p. 222)*

In this example, the criteria are listed and the rubrics are
included. (Remember that criteria handed out in advance
must be general, not task specific.) Criteria and rubrics point
the way to success, so be sure to include a rubric written in
language your students will understand. It gives them a means
to self-assess and to revise their performance or product before
turning it in. The timeline for your task may even require this
step. (In Chapter 6 we elaborate on how to use tasks and
rubrics in assessment *for* learning contexts.)

The sixth and last descriptor is a caveat about task content.
Does it script the task so tightly that the only thing you are
measuring is direction-following?

*The content of the task is sufficient to let students
know what they are to do without giving so much
information that the task will no longer measure
level of mastery of the intended learning target. The
content points the way to success without doing the
thinking for the student.*

Notice that our sample task tells students they are to use their knowledge of the physics of motion. Specifically, they will have to use their knowledge about the relation between distance and time to determine rate. If the task had told them to do that explicitly, perhaps more students would succeed. However, if the learning target to be measured requires a determination of whether students can recognize which formula to use, then telling them outright would make the results invalid. We see many tasks that, in the name of helping students succeed, give step-by-step instructions that allow students to bypass a portion of the thinking they must do to demonstrate level of proficiency on a particular target. We call this *over-scaffolding*, and it is a problem if the task is an assessment *of* learning. Highly scaffolded tasks are often useful as teaching tasks, helping students grow in their achievement. The key is to remove the scaffolding in stages so that students are able ultimately to perform independently of the help the scaffolding provides, especially if they will be required to do so on a high-stakes assessment of the learning target.

Task Quality Criterion 2: *Sampling*

This criterion only has one descriptor, but several ideas are embedded within it:

> *The number of tasks or repeated instances of performance is sufficient to measure the intended learning target and to support the kind of judgment intended to be made.*

When you evaluate the sufficiency of a sample, you ask the question, "Do I have enough evidence to support the judgment I want to make?" The answer depends on a number of factors—the complexity of the learning target, the decision the evidence will inform, proximity of the student's performance to an important cutoff mark, and consistency of the student's performance. In our discussion of these factors, we offer general guidelines, not rigid rules, for consideration. In the case of sampling, we all must exercise professional judgment in the simultaneous consideration of all factors; this is in part about the *art* of performance assessment.

Complexity of the Target

A general rule of thumb is that if the target is a simple one, it may require fewer instances—a smaller sample—to judge level of achievement. If the target is a complex one, it may require more. For example, you may be able to judge a primary student's reading rate with one or two performances. This target is relatively narrow and sharply focused. A demonstration or two will allow you to see all its dimensions. However, if you want to judge a student's proficiency at reading aloud with fluency, you may need several performances before you are confident that you have an accurate measure. This target is more complex, because more components are involved—the definition of *fluency* may include accuracy, phrasing, and expression. You may need more demonstrations just to hear and evaluate all of the parts. It may take students a few tries to put it all together. An even more complex learning target, such as "Uses mathematics to define and solve problems," will require multiple assessments, because it requires that you assess the ability to define problems and to solve them using a variety of strategies within the context of several mathematics content strands.

Decision the Evidence Will Inform

If you will use the results in a low-stakes assessment *for* learning context, the goal might be to help students see what they still need to work on. In this case, if you're wrong, you will find out right away and can make adjustments. So, one task may provide sufficient information to work from, because the consequences of an incorrect inference are small and easily corrected. If your purpose is to see and influence growth, the sample can be gathered at intervals. You and your students might examine several instances of the same performance over time looking for a pattern of growth.

In a high-stakes assessment *of* learning context, the question becomes, "What is the cost of an incorrect decision?" In other words, how high stakes is the decision? Are you deciding who passes and who fails on the basis of the results? If so, you are going to want more, rather than fewer, samples of performance to be sure you are making the correct inference about level of proficiency.

Proximity to the Cutoff Mark

When a student's level of achievement is very close to or on the dividing line between two levels of proficiency, such as very close to "meets the standard," or on the borderline between two grades, it is helpful to have more samples to justify assigning the level or grade. But when the student's performance is considerably above or below an important cutoff point, more data are not likely to change the judgment of level of achievement.

Consistency of Performance

The sampling challenge in performance assessment is gathering just enough evidence to make a relatively confident judgment of competence. A student who consistently performs at one level of proficiency leads you to a confident judgment that future performance will approximate past performance. However, erratic performance does not engender that confidence and thus requires more evidence, which will help in converging on a judgment of level of proficiency.

The decision about sufficient sample size cannot be reduced to a rule or a number. Remember, it ultimately rests on consideration of the combination of these four factors *and your own professional judgment.* You know you have enough information when you can use the evidence you have gathered to confidently predict how the student would do on the next assessment of this learning target if you were to give it.

Task Quality Criterion 3: *Distortion Due to Bias*

Even though you have designed or selected a task following the criteria discussed, things can still go wrong that can compromise the accuracy of the results. We want to avoid the circumstance where the proficient student fails to perform or the non-proficient student is judged to be performing at an acceptable level. This criterion outlines potential problems to look for.

The first descriptor refers to the instructions:

The instructions are clear and unambiguous.

Are the directions worded clearly? Are they formatted in a way that is easy to follow? Are any instructions missing? Evaluating for this descriptor is a matter of reading the directions yourself through the eyes of one of your students, perhaps one who is easily confused. Or, you might have students read the directions and then retell them in their own words. Would they know what is needed and how to proceed?

The second descriptor states whether the timeline is reasonable:

The task is narrow enough in scope to be completed successfully in the time allotted. It is clear that enough time has been allotted for successful completion of the task.

With complex tasks, it is easy to underestimate the amount of time it will take students to do a good job. If your task scores low on this descriptor, you will either have to narrow its scope (or break it into two or more tasks) or extend the timeline. Avoid the circumstance where the proficient student is not able to demonstrate proficiency due to lack of time, because the result will misrepresent the student's true state of achievement.

The third descriptor helps you think through the problems that choice of task presents:

> *If the task allows students to choose different tasks, it is clear that all choices will provide evidence of achievement on the same learning targets. All choices ask for the same performance or product, with approximately the same level of difficulty, and under the same conditions.*

If the learning target to be assessed is giving an oral presentation, such as, "The student creates a comprehensive and organized oral presentation with a clear sequencing of ideas and transitions," then it would be appropriate to offer choices in content, and perhaps in size of audience. As long as the learning target doesn't require the use of specific content or a large group as an audience, those conditions can vary. It would not be appropriate to allow students to choose between giving the presentation to an audience and turning in a written script, because only the first option can lead to an accurate measure of the intended learning target.

The fourth descriptor relates to the resources the task requires:

> *All resources required for successful completion of the task are available to all students.*

If the task requires the use of anything beyond the school's resources, you must make sure that all students have access to sufficient resources to fulfill the task requirements. If students must use the public library and some students can't get there, the task is not fair. If the task requires purchase of six mousetraps, mousetraps should be available for those students whose parents don't buy them. Otherwise, the proficient student may be misjudged for lack of opportunity to succeed.

The fifth descriptor outlines a condition that can be tricky to fulfill:

Successful completion of the task does not depend on skills unrelated to the target being measured (e.g., intensive reading in a mathematics task).

This problem arises most often when tasks involve reading and writing; many performance tasks in subjects other than Language Arts do rest in part on the ability to read and write. It is true that students with a low level of literacy are at a disadvantage with such tasks. The goal here is to minimize the impact that lack of learning in one subject has on successful task completion in another subject.

The sixth and final descriptor addresses potential cultural biases:

The task is culturally robust. Successful completion is not dependent on having had one particular cultural or linguistic background.

If the task requires use of unique or special knowledge, then students whose background does not include exposure to that knowledge will be at a disadvantage. An example is a mathematics task requiring knowledge of baseball in order to interpret statistics. If a task requires a public display of knowledge, then students whose culture frowns on calling attention to the self, especially among children, will be placed at a disadvantage. For these children, this task would be embarrassing and could lead to an inaccurate judgment of competence; they may be able but unwilling to demonstrate competence. Requiring a presentation in English of those who lack confidence in English may yield distorted results. These are problems that can be avoided if teachers remain aware of the cultural and linguistic backgrounds of their students.

Authenticity and Complexity

Authenticity and complexity are two task features often linked to quality. Authenticity, while desirable, is not always required to provide accurate information, and complexity is not always a good thing.

You can provide authenticity in part through your selection of learning targets to assess with performance assessment. Which of the targets that you teach will lend themselves best to this method of assessment? Which call for the creation of a product or performance that would be found in life beyond school? Answer these questions, and you can set up the context of the task to mirror those conditions. Sometimes, however, authenticity does not add to the quality of the task, as in the case of assessing reading rate. It is difficult to come up with a situation outside of school in which you would focus on your reading rate alone, yet many schools have a designated reading rate as a target goal for primary students and do assess it with a performance assessment.

The level of complexity of the task depends on the purpose for the assessment and the learning target(s) to be assessed. Some purposes are better served with simpler tasks. For example, if the purpose of your assessment is to provide students feedback on their current level of achievement, a series of short tasks focusing on one or two key dimensions of quality may be more useful than a single complex task. Some learning targets, while suited to performance assessment, are not complex enough to warrant a complex task. If a reasoning, performance skill, or product learning target is fairly straight-forward, a complex task may make it unnecessarily difficult for students to demonstrate mastery and may also make the results more difficult to interpret.

Although authenticity and complexity can make tasks better in many situations, we believe their inclusion hinges on the purpose for the assessment and the learning targets to be assessed, and we do not consider them to be requirements of all good tasks.

Ensuring Performance Task Quality

Ensuring performance task quality requires following the same stages of development that all other assessment methods must adhere to: planning, developing, critiquing, and administering and revising.

At the planning stage, you identify the purpose for the assessment: How will you use the information? Who else will you want to use it? What decisions will you and they make? You then identify the learning target or targets that will be the focus of the assessment. Double check that the learning targets do require a performance assessment.

Figure 4.3 Ensuring Performance Task Quality

- Plan
- Develop
- Critique
- Administer and Revise

Source: Adapted from *Classroom Assessment* for *Student Learning: Doing It Right—Using It Well* (pp. 106–117) by R. J. Stiggins, J. A. Arter, J. Chappuis, and S. Chappuis, 2004, Portland, OR: Assessment Training Institute. Adapted by permission.

Developing or selecting a performance assessment follows. You can use the *Rubric for Tasks* (Appendix D) to identify or develop a task suited to your purpose and learning target. Likewise, you can use the *Rubric for Rubrics* (Appendix A) to develop or select a rubric that will serve your intended purposes and give you accurate information about achievement on the targets you intend to assess.

We recommend that you critique your tasks and rubrics with these two scoring guides before using them with students to ensure they adhere to standards of quality. Following this, give the performance assessment and note any problems that either you or the students face. Reexamine the assessment in light of any problems that may have arisen with the task or the results, and revise as needed.

Summary

1. Creating or selecting a high-quality performance task begins with planning: first identify the purpose for the assessment and the target or targets to be assessed. All other decisions about the task flow from these two initial determinations.

2. High-quality performance tasks adhere to three criteria:

   - *Content of the Task:* The task supplies the right information to the student.

   - *Sampling:* The task provides enough evidence to support the intended use of the information.

   - *Distortion Due to Bias:* The task avoids problems that can interfere with obtaining an accurate picture of student achievement.

3. Authenticity and complexity of tasks are desirable in certain situations and not practical or desirable in others.

4. You ensure performance task quality by following these steps:

   - *Plan:* Identify the purpose for the assessment and the learning target or targets to be assessed.

   - *Develop or Select:* Use the rubric for tasks as a guideline for developing or selecting the task.

   - *Critique:* Use the rubric for tasks to check for adherence to standards of quality.

   - *Administer and Revise:* Give the task, note any problems, and revise as needed for future use.

chapter

$$\left[\ 5\ \right]$$

How to Convert Rubric Scores to Grades

There are no right grades, only justifiable grades.

—K. O'Connor
How to Grade for Learning: Linking Grades to Standards (2nd ed.),
Arlington Heights, IL: Skylight, 2002, p. 190

G rading is an assessment *of* learning event. It is a summing up, a judgment about the quality of student work or the amount a student has learned. You certainly may use rubrics for this summation. However, rubric scores don't convert directly to grades. Also, because rubrics are wonderful assessment *for* learning tools, it's important to grade so that the assessment *for* learning potential of rubrics is not diminished. The recommendations we make in this chapter support both assessment *of* and *for* learning purposes.

In this chapter we will cover the following:

1. Converting the score(s) on a single piece of work into an overall judgment of performance

2. Combining scores across work to make a summary judgment of grade or level of proficiency.

3. Combining rubric scores with percentage information from other assessments to determine a final grade or judgment of proficiency.

Note that in many countries, the term *grade* applies only to the summary of all evaluation data for a period of time. A C on a single piece of work is not called a *grade*; it is called a *mark*. In the United States, we use the term *grade* to refer to both the symbol placed on a single piece of work and to the summary of all evaluation data for a period of time; e.g., the report card *grade*. Throughout this chapter we will use the term *grade* as it is used in the United States.

Grading Caveats

Throughout this chapter we make recommendations for converting rubric scores to grades. These recommendations are based on three caveats. As we discuss them, think about how they reflect your ideas about rubrics and grading.

Caveat 1: Use Grades Only to Communicate

Why do we grade? What do we want grades to do for us? For our students? For others needing information on student learning—parents, other educators, colleges and universities, the public? The following is a list of typical reasons:

- To let students know how they did on a single piece of work, or in a subject over time.

- To communicate with others how students performed on a single piece of work, or in a subject over time.

- To make a statement about students' current level of mastery of important learning targets.

- To motivate students to try. "Let's try for As." "If you do all the work well, then you'll get an A." "If you work harder, you can meet the standard; you're almost there."

- To punish students for not trying. "If you don't try hard, and/or don't do the work well, and/or don't do all the work, and/or don't come to class, then you'll get a lower grade or fail."

We recommend that the *single* purpose for assigning grades should be to communicate, never to motivate or punish. Although grades and other judgments of adequacy do motivate some students, many students couldn't care less what grade they get. Grades for these students have ceased to serve as motivators, and can even be distinctly unmotivating. For some students it is better to have an excuse for failing — "I just didn't try"—than to try and fail once again. For these students a better way to use assessment to motivate effort is to apply assessment *for* learning strategies, which we describe in Chapter 6. If we handle motivation using assessment in this way, grades are free to serve a communication purpose.

Caveat 2: Use Grades Only to Communicate About Learning

What factors do teachers include in grades? When two sets of researchers asked teachers this question (McMillan, 2001, p. 28—secondary teachers; O'Sullivan et al., 2005, p. 35—elementary teachers), they found that almost every teacher includes academic achievement; 54 percent include zeros for work not completed; 30 to 80 percent include such nonacademic factors as effort, class participation, and ability; and 10 to 20 percent include such nonacademic factors as behavior and attendance. These results are supported by other researchers (Cicmanec, Johanson, & Howley, 2001) who asked secondary math teachers what they included in their grades. Respondents stated that they based grades 86 percent on academic learning, and 14 percent on nonacademic factors such as ability, effort, and participation.

We recommend that the *only* factor included in grades be academic learning. This recommendation is supported by other grading experts (e.g., Brookhart, 2004; Guskey, 1996; Guskey & Bailey, 2001; O'Connor, 2002; Stiggins et al., 2004). Effort and behavior are important, but should be reported and dealt with separately. If they are not reported separately, it is impossible to interpret a grade's meaning and it therefore loses its ability to communicate. It is difficult enough to ensure that grades are comparable among different classrooms when they are based only on student learning; put in other factors, defined and weighted differently, and it becomes almost impossible. (For an in-depth examination of the types of information to include in grades and the relationship between assessment and student motivation, see Stiggins et al., 2004, especially Chapter 10; and Stiggins & O'Connor, 2006.)

Caveat 3: Grades Are Not the Best Way to Give Students Feedback on Learning

The first purpose for grading that we listed at the beginning of this discussion is to communicate to students about how they did. Grades, by definition, represent assessments *of* learning. Their usefulness as feedback to learners is limited. To promote learning and minimize unintended negative side effects, feedback needs both to point out what was done well and to indicate the next steps in learning. Evaluative feedback—whether A, B, C, D, F; ✓⁺, ✓, ✓⁻; ☺, ☺, ☹; or *exceeds standard, meets standard, approaches standard, below standard*—cannot provide such detailed information. Rubric scores and their attached descriptors function far better as feedback.

The caveats, listed in Figure 5.1, lead to our first two recommendations on rubrics and grading:

> *Recommendation 1:* Use grades only to communicate about student learning.

> *Recommendation 2:* Do not convert rubric scores to grades until you must provide assessment *of* learning information. Use rubrics to provide descriptive feedback to students during learning. Assess a lot; grade a little.

Assigning a Grade to a Single Piece of Work Scored with a Rubric

Don't Use Percentages, Use a Logic Rule

Consider the three examples in Figure 5.2.

Look at the achievement levels assigned to each criteria in the three examples in the figure. What grade would you give to each piece of work? Many teachers would give the following:

- Example 1: B– or C+
- Example 2: A– or B+
- Example 3: B– or C+

Figure 5.1 Grading Caveats

1. Grades should be used *only* to communicate.
2. Grades should be used only to communicate *about learning*.
3. Grades are not the best way to give students feedback on learning.

Converting rubric scores directly to percentages and then to grades is tempting, but flawed. Let us see why. Here is what happens:

Example 1:

Convert each score to a percentage:
4 / 5 = 80%, 3 / 5 = 60%, 4 / 5 = 80%, 3 / 5 = 60%, 2 / 5 = 40%.

Determine the average percentage:
(80 + 60 + 80 + 60 + 40) / 5 = 320 / 5 = 64%

Convert average percentage to a grade:
64% = D

Example 2:

Convert each score to a percentage:
4 / 4 = 100%, 3 / 4 = 75%, 4 / 4 = 100%, 2/ 4 = 50%,
3 / 4 = 75%

Determine the average percentage:
(100 + 75 + 100 + 50 + 75) / 5 = 400 / 5 = 80%

Convert the average percentage to a grade:
80% = B– or C+

Example 3:

Convert the score to a percentage:
4 / 6 = 67%

Convert the percentage to a grade:
67% = D

Why don't these percentage procedures match the initial judgments? The reason is that *percentages don't accurately represent level of learning as measured by a rubric.* For example, on a four-level rubric the only percentages possible are 100, 75, 50, and 25. These would be A, C, F, and F. The descriptors at level 3 probably don't match C-level work, and the descriptors at level 2 probably don't describe failing work. On a five-point scale the only percentages possible are 100, 80, 60, 40, and 20. These might convert to A, B–/C+, F, F, and F. Once again, descriptors at level 4 probably don't describe B–/C+ work, and descriptors at level 3 probably don't describe failing work.

Therefore, resist the temptation to base grades on calculating the percentage of possible rubric points. Instead, look at the descriptions of the various levels and decide on direct conversions from rubric scores to grades without first converting to percentages. We call this *using a logic rule* because you must determine logically how the descriptions in a rubric relate to the grades A, B, C, D, and F. Table 5.1 shows possible logic rules for converting performance on a single piece of work to a grade. Your logic rule will depend on the wording in your own rubric.

Note that in Table 5.1 some rubric scores are reported as decimals. This occurs in analytic rubrics when the several criterion scores are averaged. The six-level holistic rubric has only a single criterion, so no averaging is possible. Instead, there is a one-to-one conversion between the rubric and a grade.

Let's consider the grade we'd give each piece of student work in Figure 5.2, using the logic rules in Table 5.1.

Figure 5.2 Sample Scores on a Single Piece of Student Work

Example 1: Analytic Rubric with 5 Criteria and 5 Levels

	5	4	3	2	1
Criterion A score		•			
Criterion B score			•		
Criterion C score		•			
Criterion D score			•		
Criterion E score				•	

Overall Grade? _____

Example 2: Analytic Rubric with 5 Criteria and 4 Levels

	4	3	2	1
Criterion A score	•			
Criterion B score		•		
Criterion C score	•			
Criterion D score			•	
Criterion E score		•		

Overall Grade? _____

Example 3: Holistic Rubric with 6 Levels

	6	5	4	3	2	1
Score			•			

Table 5.1 Sample Logic Rules for Converting Rubric Scores to Grades on a Single Piece of Student Work

Example 1: Five-Level, Six-Trait Writing Rubric		Example 2: Four-Level Analytic Rubric		Example 3: Six-Level Holistic Rubric	
Grade	*Average Rubric Score*	*Grade*	*Average Rubric Score*	*Grade*	*Rubric Score*
A	4.2 and above	A	3.5–4.0	A	6
B	3.5–4.1	B	3.0–3.4	B	5
C	2.8–3.4	C	2.5–2.9	C	3 or 4
D	2.0–2.7	D	1.5–2.4	D	2
F	1.9 and below	F	1.0–1.4	F	1

Source: Example 1 is adapted from *Creating Writers: Through 6-Trait Writing Assessment and Instruction* (p. 363) by V. Spandel, 2005, Boston: Allyn & Bacon. Copyright ©2005 by Allyn & Bacon. All rights reserved. Adapted by permission.

Example 1 in Figure 5.2 (five criteria and five levels):

Average rubric score = (4 + 3 + 4 + 3 + 2) / 5 = 16 / 5 = 3.2

Convert the average score to a grade using Example 1, Table 5.1: 3.2 = C+

Example 2 in Figure 5.2 (five criteria and four levels):

Average rubric score = (4 + 3 + 4 + 2 + 3) / 5 = 16 / 5 = 3.2

Convert the average score to a grade using Example 2, Table 5.1: 3.2 = B

Example 3 in Figure 5.2:

There is only a single score since the rubric is holistic = 4

Convert the score to a grade using Example 3, Table 5.1: 4 = C+

The purpose of the logic rule is to consistently give the same grade to the same range of quality. This discussion leads to our third recommendation for converting rubric scores to grades.

> *Recommendation 3:* Do not convert rubric scores to percentages (number of points earned divided by number of points possible) to determine a grade. Average the rubric scores themselves and convert that average to a grade using a logic rule.

Remember, the scores for the analytic rubrics were averaged across criteria for grading purposes (assessment *of* learning) only. For assessment *for* learning purposes, maintaining discrete criterion ratings preserves the link to descriptive detail about student strengths and weaknesses.

Recall also that although you have an analytic rubric you don't necessarily need to consider all criteria for every piece of work. In fact, when students are practicing, it is useful to practice on each criterion category separately and, when the time comes to grade such work, you can base the grade on only the criteria being emphasized.

Suggestions for Creating a Logic Rule

Educator Vicki Spandel noticed that taking a straight percentage of number of points earned divided by total number of possible points leads to grades that don't make sense. Here is the calculation for Example 1 in Figure 5.2:

Number of points earned: 4 + 3 + 4 + 3 + 2 = 16

Number of points possible: 5 criteria times 5 levels = 25

Percentage of points earned out of points possible:
16 / 25 = 64%

Here is how she developed her own logic rule (see Example 1 in Table 5.1, and see Table 5.2): "Grades are actually arbitrary more than scientific [and are] based largely on teacher instinct.

What I discovered was that straight conversion (e.g., 3 is 60% of 5) led to abysmally low scores and grades that didn't mesh with common sense. A person who routinely gets 3s on a 5-point scale is not blowing anyone's socks off, true, but she is not on the verge of failing either. Something was clearly wrong. I finally realized it was the nature of the continuum that required us to adjust the math a bit.

"I add .5 to each [average score]. For example, let's say a student has a 3.8. I add .5 to this, making it 4.3. OK—then dividing 4.3 by 5 gives us .86, or 86%. That's a solid B for most teachers, and that's just what the chart says" (personal communication, 2006).

Developing a logic rule has not been standardized. However, people who develop them follow these general guidelines:

1. Work with others!

2. Examine your rubric and samples of student work. Make judgments about which score averages should convert to which grades based on your experience as a teacher. (Use the samples in Table 5.1 as departure points for your own experimentation.)

3. Apply your draft logic rule to a new collection of student work. Adjust the rule as needed until your grades reflect your professional judgment.

How to Weight Rubric Scores

Our examples so far have averaged the rubric scores for each criterion straight across the board—each is weighted the same. You also can, of course, give some criteria more weight than others. For example, let's say you have a rubric with three criteria and four levels and you want to weight the first criterion twice as much as the other two. Assume the first criterion score is 3, the second criterion score is 2, and the third criterion score is 4. You would multiply the first criterion score by 2 to give it the desired weight and then add it to the others to get a total score: $(2 \times 3) + 2 + 4 = 12$. Next, divide the total by the number of scores: $12 / 4 = 3.00$.

Using the logic rule in Table 5.1 for the four-level analytic rubric (Example 2), the grade would be a B. If this seems high or low to you based on your rubrics and experience, you need to create a different logic rule.

Table 5.2 Sample Logical Percentage Equivalent Table for Combining Rubric Scores with Percentage Scores

Average Rubric Score	Grade Conversion	Logical Percentage Equivalent[1]
4.8–5.0	A+	98
4.5–4.7	A	95
4.2–4.4	A–	91
4.0–4.1	B+	88
3.8–3.9	B	85
3.5–3.7	B–	81
3.2–3.4	C+	78
3.0–3.1	C	75
2.8–2.9	C–	71
2.5–2.7	D+	68
2.2–2.4	D	65
2.0–2.1	D–	61
1.0–1.9	F	59

[1]Taken from a school district's table for converting percentages to grades.

Source: The first two columns are adapted from *Creating Writers: Through 6-Trait Writing Assessment and Instruction* (p. 363) by V. Spandel, 2005, Boston: Allyn & Bacon. Copyright ©2005 by Allyn & Bacon. All rights reserved. Adapted by permission.

Determining a Final Grade Across Several Pieces of Work, All Scored Using a Rubric

When determining the final grade for a grading period, the goal is to sum up achievement as accurately as possible.

As an example, consider Figure 5.3, which shows Lee's scores in writing over a semester using the *6 + 1 Trait™ Writing Assessment Scoring Guide* (in Appendix C and on the CD). The first half of the papers were persuasive writing and the second half were expository. Note that not all traits were evaluated for every piece of work; some assignments were designed to emphasize only a couple of traits (dashes indicate those traits not evaluated). Also, note that Lee did not turn in assignment 9.

What final grade would you give Lee? What would you take into consideration when assigning the final grade? Consider these issues:

- Because writing is a cumulative skill that develops over time, should all papers count in the final grade or judgment of mastery? If not, how many should be used to get the most accurate picture of current achievement across types of writing?

- If scores on all the papers are to be used, should the missing scores on assignment 9 be counted as zeros?

- Should any of the criteria be weighted more than the others? For example, should *Ideas*, *Organization*, and *Conventions* count more than *Voice*, *Word Choice*, and *Sentence Fluency*?

- Were some of the papers practice? If so, should they be used at all?

Let's see how these different decisions affect the calculation of Lee's final grade. Because Lee's writing was scored using the *6-Trait* writing rubric, we will use Spandel's logic rule from Table 5.1 (Example 1).

If we decide to use all scores and count zero for the four scores on the missing paper:

Rubric score total / number of rubric scores = average score = 198 / 59 = 3.36 = C+

Figure 5.3 Lee's Writing Scores Using the 6-Trait Writing Rubric

The *6 + 1 Trait™ Writing Assessment Scoring Guide* has six criteria, called *traits*, and five levels. Therefore, each score in the table below represents the number of points obtained out of five possible. The first six assignments were persuasive writing; the second six were expository (informational) writing.

Trait Assignment	Ideas	Organization	Voice	Word Choice	Sentence Fluency	Conventions
1. Persuasive	2	—	—	—	—	3
2. Persuasive	2	3	2	1	—	2
3. Persuasive	5	4	—	—	4	4
4. Persuasive	4	4	4	2	3	4
5. Persuasive	4	4	3	3	3	4
6. Persuasive	5	4	5	4	4	5
7. Expository	3	2	—	—	—	4
8. Expository	3	3	4	3	—	4
9. Expository	missing	missing	—	—	missing	missing
10. Expository	5	3	3	3	4	5
11. Expository	5	4	3	3	5	3
12. Expository	5	5	3	4	4	4

1. Using all papers, counting missing work as 0; average = 198 / 59 = 3.36 = C+

2. Using all papers except the missing paper; average = 198 / 55 = 3.6 = B–

3. Using the final two papers from each type of writing (nos. 5, 6, 11, 12) = 96 / 24 = 4.0 = B+

If we decide to use all scores and do not count zero for the four scores on the missing paper:

Rubric score total / number of rubric scores = average score = 198 / 55 = 3.6 = B–

If we decide to use all the scores on only the final two papers of each type of writing:

Rubric score total / number of rubric scores = average score = 96 / 24 = 4.0 = B+

Which of these grades best represents Lee's level of *achievement* as of the end of the grading period? We would say the third one does.

Counting missing work as zero unfairly weights a single missing piece of work. For example, if Lee's scores were 5, 5, 0, 0, 5, 5, 0, 5, 5, 5, 5, and 5, the average would be 45 / 12 = 3.8 = B. Does a B best represent his achievement or is it better to conclude that the evidence points to an A? It takes a lot of fives to make up for a single zero. Also, are we using grades to punish students for not turning in work or are we trying to sum up student status most accurately? Finally, does a B tell anyone that Lee is missing work? If missing work is a problem, it should be dealt with directly, and separately.

If there is enough evidence of achievement—you don't need the missing work—to make a summative judgment, calculate the grade without it. If there is not enough evidence of achievement to make an accurate summation of student achievement, then you need more data. Perhaps consider the scores on an additional paper, such as paper 8. Or, tell students that you'll drop out their lowest score and average the rest. Or, use practice work as extra evidence.

This discussion leads to two more recommendations.

Recommendation 4: Do not factor missing work into the grade.

Recommendation 5: When the achievement is cumulative over time, base the grade on the most recent work.

Misconception Alert
Do You *Always* Use the Most Current Work?

The type of learning targets for which general rubrics are appropriate are reasoning proficiencies, performance skills, or products—where expertise develops over time. We recommend using the most up-to-date evidence to sum up achievement on such targets. In these situations, for the same learning target, it makes no sense to count beginning work equally with more advanced work, produced when the student has become more sophisticated through practice.

However, not all learning targets develop over time. Students sometimes must learn distinct units of material. This most commonly occurs with knowledge learning targets. For example, in sixth grade, the first science unit might be the solar system, and the second might be ecology, and so on. There is a different body of knowledge for each that is independent of the next. It is acceptable to average the scores from discrete targets such as these throughout the grading period; there may be no later information to consider.

Combining Rubric Scores with Percentage Scores to Determine a Final Grade

The final situation we discuss is when the record of student achievement during a grading period includes some rubric scores and some test scores using percentages. You can't combine them directly because percentages encompass score points from 0 to 100 and rubric scores encompass score points, for example, from 1 to 5. And you can't convert the rubric scores directly to percentages because, as we discussed previously, your results will misrepresent student achievement. Instead, we recommend using a logic rule for converting rubric scores to *logical percentages*.

Step 1: Average the Ratings on the Rubric Portion of the Grade

First, as in the previous section, average the ratings on the rubric portion of the grade. This presumes that you've already decided (1) which work represents the most current level of performance, (2) not to count missing work as zero, and (3) which assignments or rubric criteria are to be weighted more or less than others.

For example, the average rating on Lee's final two papers of each type of writing was calculated to be 4.0 by adding all scores for the final two papers of each type of writing (total = 96) and then dividing by the number of scores (6 scores x 4 papers = 24).

Step 2: Convert to a Logical Percentage

At this point convert the average rating to a *logical percentage*, as shown in Table 5.2; we aren't ready for a grade yet. For Lee's average rubric score of 4.0, the logical percentage equivalent is 88 percent.

Note that the first two columns in Table 5.2 (*Average Rubric Score* and corresponding *Grade Conversion*) comprise an expanded version of the logic rule table shown in Table 5.1, Example 1. Here's the clever part: The last column in Table 5.2

(the logical percentages) is each *Grade Conversion*'s percentage equivalent, which you would take right from your district's regular percentage-to-grade conversion chart. This juxtaposition allows you to logically convert an average rubric score to a percentage so that you can combine it with percentage scores from other tests.

Variation on the Theme
Logic Rule Example 4

Here is another option for a logic rule that teachers have found useful. With this approach, Lee's performance on all the papers would be a C with or without counting the missing papers as zeros. Lee's performance on the final four papers would be a B. You must experiment and decide which logic rule gives *you* the most accurate results. Remember, the purpose of the logic rule is to consistently give the same grade to the same range of work.

Grade	Pattern of Rubric Scores
A	At least 50% of the scores are 5. No more than 10% of the scores are below 4.
B	At least 20% of the scores are 5. At least 50% of the scores are 4. No more than 20% of the scores are below 4.
C	At least 20% of the scores are 4 or 5. No more than 20% of the scores are below 3.
D	At least 20% of the scores are 3 or above. No more than 50% of the scores are 1.
F	More than 50% of the scores are 1.

Step 3: Decide on the Weight for Each Portion of the Grade and Compute the Average Percentage

Assume that the percentage portion of Lee's grade is 80. Will the rubric portion be weighted the same as the percentage portion? Less? More? Assume that you decided to weight both percentages the same. The final grade will be found by adding together the percentage portion of the grade (80%) and the logical percentage of the rubric portion of the grade (88%) and dividing by two:

$$(80 + 88) / 2 = 84\%$$

Now, let's say you decided to weight the percentage portion of the grade twice as much as the rubric portion. You would first multiply the first percentage by 2 to give it the desired weight and then add it to the logical percentage from the rubric portion:

$$(2 \times 80) + 88 = 248$$

Next, divide the total by the number of scores:

$$248 / 3 = 82.7\%$$

Step 4: Convert the Average Percentage to a Grade

If the two portions of the grade are weighted the same, the average percentage is 84 percent. This would correspond to a B using the conversion table in Table 5.2.

If the two portions of the grade are weighted as shown previously, the average percentage is 82.7 percent. This corresponds to a B– using the conversion table in Table 5.2.

This process illustrates our sixth recommendation:

Recommendation 6: When combining rubric information with percentage information from other assessments, use a logic rule to convert the rubric score average to a logical percentage before combining.

Summary

We make the following recommendations for converting rubric scores to grades:

1. Use grades *only* to communicate about *student learning.*

2. Do not convert rubric scores to grades unless you must. Use rubrics to provide descriptive feedback to students *during* learning. Assess a lot; grade a little.

3. Do not convert rubric scores to percentages (number points earned divided by total number of points possible) and then to grades. Average the rubric scores and convert the average to a grade using a logic rule.

4. Do not factor missing work into the grade.

5. When the achievement is cumulative over time, base the grade on the most recent work.

6. When combining rubric information with percentage information from other assessments, calculate the average rubric score and convert this to a percentage using a logical percentage based on your logic rule. Combine this logical percentage equivalent with the other percentage information and use your district's percentage-to-grade conversion table to designate the final grade.

chapter

$$\left[\, \mathbf{6} \, \right]$$

Tasks and Rubrics as Assessment *for* Learning

Can assessment raise standards? Recent research has shown that the answer to this question is an unequivocal "yes." Assessment is one of the most powerful educational tools for promoting effective learning. But it must be used in the right way. There is no evidence that increasing the amount of testing will enhance learning. Instead the focus needs to be on helping teachers use assessment, as part of teaching and learning, in ways that will raise pupils' achievement.

—**Assessment Reform Group**
Assessment for Learning: Beyond the Black Box,
Cambridge, UK: University of Cambridge School of Education, 1999, p. 2

Imagine a group of 9-year-olds who have signed up for their first basketball team. The coaches schedule 12 games. During the first game, they notice that many of the children don't know how to dribble, some don't know how to pass, most can't shoot, and a few aren't sure which basket is theirs. So, the coaches shout directions to the players in hopes that they will improve, and they pull a few out of the game to show them what to do. Then before the next game, they remind their players what they told them about dribbling, passing, and shooting.

That never happens, does it? At least not in basketball. The coaches of a novice team may schedule 10 or more practices before the season starts, and then continue having practices during the season. Over the course of a season, the ratio of practices to games may be 3 or 4 to 1. This scenario, however, *can* happen in the classroom. When the performance assessment that counts for a grade (the equivalent of a basketball game) is the only opportunity students have to practice, when the only teaching or feedback they get is delivered during the graded event, we are doing the same thing as teaching basketball by scheduling games.

Performance Assessments as Episodes of Learning

In the context of performance assessment, opportunity to practice and improve can be configured several ways. You can set up one or more practice tasks, use the rubric to give students feedback on their strengths and areas to work on, and let them revise their performance or product before assigning the task you will grade. This often works well with performance tasks that don't take days or weeks to complete. For example, in mathematics you can use several tasks, all assessing the same learning target, as practice. On the first task, offer students feedback, based on the rubric you will use, to show them what they are doing well and what they still need to master. On the second task, let them give each other feedback based on the rubric. On the third task, have them use the rubric to self-assess. Then use the fourth task as the graded event. Many states in the United States offer practice tasks that mirror the state test. Rather than using them solely as graded events, you may want to use them in a progression such as this.

Remember from Chapter 5 that when figuring a final grade you want to use a representative sample of the student's *most recent achievement* on each learning target. So, while you may assign a grade to a number of tasks (but not to all of them!), you may, in the final analysis, use a smaller number of the more recent tasks to figure the final grade.

On a more lengthy assignment, such as a science laboratory experiment report, you may want to break the task into smaller pieces. Students can write just the hypothesis and receive feedback on it, based on the rubric that will be used to grade the report. Or you may give them a different experiment context, have them draft a hypothesis, and revise it using the rubric-based feedback from you, from other students, or from a self-assessment before tackling the whole lab report. You can follow the same procedure for any other parts of the report that students may need more practice with before demonstrating their achievement.

Figure 6.1 Performance Tasks as Practice

- Schedule feedback, self-assessment, and revision on short practice tasks before the assessment *of* learning.

- Break complex task into parts and schedule feedback, self-assessment, and revision on each part before students put them together for the assessment *of* learning.

- Schedule feedback, self-assessment, and revision multiple times while students are developing a complex performance or product to be used as an assessment *of* learning.

Another approach, used often in English classes, is to use the same task as assessment *for* and assessment *of* learning by engaging students in a writing process such as that illustrated in Figure 6.2. Here the teacher assigns a lengthy paper and gives students time to assemble their ideas and organize them into a draft. Students share their drafts with peers and receive feedback focused on one or more criteria from the rubric. In writing, for example, if the instruction is focused on the two traits of *Ideas and Content* and *Voice*, students' feedback to each other would also focus on *Ideas and Content* and *Voice*. Students then use this feedback as well as their own thoughts to revise the draft. They may repeat the draft/feedback/self-assess/revise cycle several times before submitting the paper to the teacher for feedback. Last, students revise their writing based on the teacher's feedback and turn the paper in for a grade. This process approach can also be used for shorter practice pieces, where students work on improving a paper for a selected number of criteria as explained, and then put the paper into a working folder. At a later date, students choose one piece from their writing folders to develop further and then turn it in for a grade, as an assessment *of* learning.

Rubrics as Teaching Tools

Using performance tasks as assessments *for* learning requires that students be familiar with the rubric that will be used to evaluate the final performance or product. Handing the rubric out in advance and asking students to read it is, more often than not, insufficient. With a little advance planning, a good rubric can be an effective and versatile teaching tool; with the right followup, it can enhance learning over the long term.

We have compiled a list of seven strategies that lay out what you can do in the classroom to incorporate assessment *for* learning into daily teaching activities (Figure 6.3). The strategies (adapted here with permission from Stiggins et al., 2004, pp. 231–240) synthesize research-based assessment practices known to improve student achievement. They are designed to introduce the rubric to students in a way that develops their understanding of the concepts of quality behind the words, and to use the rubric to do the following:

- Provide meaningful feedback that fosters student improvement.
- Offer language for students to use when self-assessing.
- Point the way toward productive revision.
- Help students notice, track, and report on their own growth.

Figure 6.2 The Writing Process as Assessment for Learning

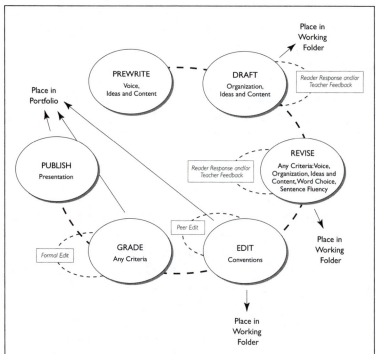

Figure 6.3 Seven Strategies of Assessment for Learning

Where Am I Going?

Strategy 1:   Provide a clear and understandable vision of the learning target.

Strategy 2:   Use examples and models of strong and weak performances or products.

Where Am I Now?

Strategy 3:   Offer regular descriptive feedback.

Strategy 4:   Teach students to self-assess and set goals.

How Can I Close the Gap?

Strategy 5:   Design lessons to focus on one aspect of quality at a time.

Strategy 6:   Teach students focused revision.

Strategy 7:   Engage students in self-reflection and let them keep track of and share their learning.

Source: Adapted from *Classroom Assessment* for *Student Learning: Doing It Right—Using It Well* (pp. 231–240) by R. J. Stiggins, J. A. Arter, J. Chappuis, and S. Chappuis, 2004, Portland, OR: Assessment Training Institute. Adapted by permission.

Strategy 1: Provide a Clear and Understandable Vision of the Learning Target

Anything you do to help students answer the question, "What are the elements of quality in the performance or product I am to create?" applies to Strategy 1. Many teachers use a version of the following steps to introduce the concepts of the rubric they will be using. In this example, we will introduce students to the language of a rubric for oral presentations:

1. Ask students what makes a good oral presentation. Record all responses on chart paper.

2. Show one or two clips of oral presentations. Ask students if they are reminded of anything else to add to the list (from Step 1). Record additional responses.

3. Tell students that this is a good list, and that they have done exactly what teachers and other content area experts do when they are creating a rubric to judge quality oral presentations. Tell them that their list includes many of the same characteristics as are on the experts' list.

4. Show them a list of the criteria represented in your rubric. For oral presentations, this might be *Content, Organization, Delivery*, and *Language*. Then show a bulleted list of the main features of each criterion, as represented in the descriptors. The bulleted list for *Content* could look like this:

   • Sticks to the topic

   • Includes interesting, informative, accurate details

   • Suits the audience and situation

   Ask students to see if any of the ideas from the bulleted list show up on their list. If there is a match, write the criterion next to the word or phrase on their chart. If there are no matches, tell students they will be learning more about *Content* later. Do the same for all of the criteria in your rubric. In going through this process, students identify what they already know, link their descriptions of quality to the language of the scoring guide, and realize that the concepts on the rubric are not totally foreign to them.

5. Hand out a version of the rubric written in language your students will understand.

Strategy 2: Use Examples and Models of Strong and Weak Performances or Products

Anything you do to help students answer the questions, "What does quality look like? What are some problems to avoid?" applies to Strategy 2. Even though you have introduced the language of the rubric to students, they still need to practice with it to understand what the descriptors mean and to be able to differentiate among different levels of quality. We recommend that, if the performance or product is complex, you focus on one criterion at a time. You may use the following procedure:

1. Select a criterion to focus on. Have students read the rubric for that criterion, beginning with the descriptors at the strong end of the scale, then reading the descriptors at the weak end of the scale, and last reading through the middle descriptors.

2. Show or give them an anonymous strong example of the performance or product. Don't tell them that it is strong. In the case of oral presentations, you could show a videotaped speech. (Note that in some contexts, such as with mathematics problem solving, this process works better if students are asked to solve the problem in the example on their own before looking at sample solutions.)

3. Ask students to put the performance or product mentally into one of two piles—strong or weak—for the criterion specified. Tell them this is silent, independent work. Have them begin reading the rubric at the appropriate end of the scale—if it is in the strong pile, they begin reading at the strong end of the scale; if it is in the weak pile, they begin reading at the weak end of the scale. If they believe it is strong, but the highest level doesn't describe it exactly, they are to read down through the levels until they find descriptors that match their judgment. Conversely, if they believe it is weak, but the lowest level doesn't describe it exactly, they are to read up through the levels until they find descriptors that most closely match their judgment. This is again independent work.

4. Students are now ready to share their judgments and reasons in small groups. Ask them to be sure to refer to the language of the rubric when explaining why they gave the example a particular rating. They do not need to come to consensus on a rating, but they should all share their judgments and reasons for them. Students can change their ratings if the discussion causes them to rethink their judgment and reasons.

5. Next, ask students to share their ratings by voting. In the case of a 5-point scale, you would ask them, "How many of you gave this example a 5?" and tally the votes. Do the same for each score or rating point in descending order. Then ask, "What did you give it and why?" The previous steps have been leading to this discussion—it is the most important part. Let students share their ratings and reasons. Remind them to refer to the language of the rubric in justifying their judgments. The point of this step is not to make sure students all center on the rating you have in mind. Rather, the purpose is to give them practice at matching examples to levels of quality as defined in the rubric, which is a necessary precursor to self-assessment.

6. You can share the rating you would give the example, if you like, but don't spend too much time explaining your own analysis at this point, even if it is widely discrepant from some or all of their judgments. Rather, select another example, this time one that is fairly weak, and follow the same procedure. Select subsequent samples to reflect problems your students typically have. Students will come to a closer convergence with your vision of quality through engaging in this activity several times.

Strategy 3: Offer Regular Descriptive Feedback

Anything you do to help students answer the questions, "What are my strengths with respect to elements of quality? What do I still need to work on? Where did I go wrong and what can I do about it?" applies to Strategy 3, and gives students information they need to improve.

Research on Effective Feedback

There has been extensive research over the last 25 years on the impact of feedback on student learning. We can think of it as a mirror; what we choose to reflect to students can either improve student learning or have a counterproductive

Misconception Alert

Shouldn't We Use Only Samples of Strong Work?

We don't think anyone would disagree with using samples of strong performances or products in assessment *for* learning contexts. However, you may question the usefulness of showing students midrange or weak examples. Such examples can be effective because they train students to look for certain problems, which helps when they are later expected to assess and revise their own work. They also help students refine their vision of exactly what quality does and doesn't look like. Consider the following when selecting samples:

- Look for several examples of work for each level of quality on each criterion. If you provide only one strong sample, students are more likely to model their performance exactly after that model. We know of a classroom in which the teacher showed one strong model that began, "I see you there, Martin Blake, your wild hair blowing in the wind." Every subsequent student paper began with the phrase, "I see you there. . . ." Showing a single strong example might be good if you want students to practice with a specific opening or sentence structure, but it would not be good if they generalize it; e.g., if every student ends up thinking, "I should open my paper with the phrase, 'I see you there . . .'"

- Select samples that represent problems students typically have. Here you do want them to generalize; identifying sample problems helps them to recognize similar occurrences in their own work, and leads them to learn how to avoid some problems altogether.

- Try to find samples that have been scored previously with the rubric you are using, or with a very similar rubric. Many times, you can find such samples annotated with explanations of why the piece received the scores it did.

effect. Some forms of feedback cause students to avoid rather than grapple with challenges, or even to give up entirely rather than push on. Because providing students with feedback about themselves as learners is time consuming, it is important that we not waste the effort. The following conclusions about effective feedback are based on this research:

- Effective feedback points out successes and gives specific information about how to improve the performance or product (Black & Wiliam, 1998; Bloom, 1984; Brown, 1994).

- Feedback is effective when it offers information about progress relative to the intended learning goal and about what action to take to reach that goal (Hattie & Timperley, 2005).

- Comments directed to the quality of the work—what was done well and what needs improving—increase student interest in the task and level of achievement (Butler, 1988).

- When teachers substitute comments for grades, students engage more productively in improving their work (Black et al., 2002).

- Grading every piece of work is misdirected. A numerical grade does not show students how to improve their work. Further, students ignore comments when grades are given (Black et al., 2002; Butler, 1988).

- Intensive correction, where the teacher marks every error in every paper a student writes, is no more effective in causing student growth than marking none of them (Hillocks, 1986).

- Feedback that describes characteristics of the learner is less effective than feedback that describes characteristics of the work (Hattie & Timperley, 2005).

- Frequently feedback is used to push students to "do more" or "do better," without being specific enough to help students know what to do. This type of feedback is generally ineffective (Hattie & Timperley, 2005).

- Feedback is effective when it addresses partial understanding. When student work demonstrates lack of understanding, feedback will not help (Hattie & Timperley, 2005).

The rubric can function completely or in part as the basis for your feedback. If students have practiced with examples of varying quality, they are familiar with what the language of the rubric means, which allows you to use words and phrases from it in your comments to them. One relatively quick way to do this is to highlight the words and phrases on the rubric matching the level of quality of their performance or product and simply hand back the highlighted rubric. You may need to include a pointer or two about how to improve the performance or product; the language from the top level of your rubric can guide you, in that it describes what high quality looks like. Make sure that you schedule time, either in or out of class, for students to act on your feedback and to prepare a revision before evaluating their work for a grade. A crucial feature of effective feedback is that it occurs while there is still time to do something about it.

Students can provide descriptive feedback to each other as well, if they have had practice describing strengths and weaknesses in anonymous samples. (For more information on preparing students to offer feedback to each other, see Stiggins et al., 2004, pp. 236–239, 363–366.)

Strategy 4: Teach Students to Self-Assess and Set Goals

Strategy 4 includes anything students do to identify where they are with respect to mastery of the desired learning and to set goals for improvement. Black and Wiliam (1998) assert that for assessment to bring about learning gains, it has to include student self-assessment. As a result of their synthesis of research on the effects of formative assessment on achievement, they state that "self-assessment by the students is not an interesting option or luxury; it has to be seen as essential" (p. 55). In performance assessments, you can ask students to use the rubric to identify their own strengths and areas for improvement. If you have given them descriptive feedback based on the rubric, you have modeled for them the kind of thinking they are to do when self-assessing. You can teach them to set specific, achievement-related goals and to make a plan to accomplish them. (For more information on goal setting and action planning with students, see Stiggins et al., 2004, pp. 367–374.)

Strategy 5: Design Lessons to Focus on One Aspect of Quality at a Time

Any time you narrow the focus of your lessons to help students master a specific knowledge, reasoning, performance skill, or product target, or to address specific misconceptions or problems, you are using your judgment to tailor teaching to specific needs. Students who are not yet proficient at creating a complex performance or product have a difficult time improving simultaneously on all elements of quality. This strategy suggests that you may want to teach lessons that address your rubric one criterion at a time. In some instances, you may need to focus on only one *part* of one criterion at a time. For example, a writing rubric might have a criterion called *Organization*. Within that criterion are descriptors about the quality of the introduction, the sequencing of ideas, transitions between ideas, pacing, and the conclusion. If your students are not writing effective and inviting introductions to their papers, give them some practice with that single aspect of the whole rubric. You could use Strategies 1 through 3: Ask "What makes a good introduction?"; share examples of strong and weak introductions; have students write an introduction to something they are working on; and offer descriptive feedback based on strengths and weaknesses of introductions as described in your rubric.

Strategy 6: Teach Students Focused Revision

Any activity that allows students to revise their initial work with a focus on a manageable number of aspects of quality, problems, or learning targets is a logical next step after teaching focused lessons. Alternatively, let them create a revision plan, detailing the steps they would take to improve their product or performance, and let that stand in for the actual revision. This is especially useful in an assessment *for* learning context; students can think about revision more frequently, because each instance takes less time. Strategy 6 gives students practice using the rubric to self-assess and to guide their revisions. When they do this it is the students and not you who are doing the thinking about and the work of revision; this translates into deeper learning.

Misconception Alert
Student Self-Grading

Student self-assessment is *not* synonymous with students assigning themselves grades. Keep in mind the difference between the assessment *for* learning context and the assessment *of* learning context. Student self-assessment is an assessment *for* learning strategy, in which students identify their own strengths and areas for improvement. Grading for reporting purposes is an assessment *of* learning activity, and is the responsibility of the teacher.

Strategy 7: Engage Students in Self-Reflection and Let Them Keep Track of and Share Their Learning

Anything you have students do that allows them to look back on their journey—to see where they've been and how far they've come—helps students develop insights into themselves as learners. Figure 6.4 is an example of a student's self-reflection, in which we clearly see the language of the rubric the class has been learning to use: "I think my writing has a lot more voice now. Voice is the part of your writing that shows how you feel about your topic because the thoughts and feelings come from your heart." Also, anything you have students do to track their learning, to summarize it, and to share it with others reinforces the learning and develops in them a sense of ownership. These activities cause students to learn more deeply and to remember it longer. (For more information about how to help students engage in self-reflection, see Stiggins et al., 2004, pp. 345–348. For more about having students track and share their learning, see the chapters on portfolios [11, pp. 335–359] and student-involved conferences [12, pp. 361–384].)

Figure 6.4 Sixth Grade Self-Reflection

I have become a better writer this year. I have learned to put more focus in my writing and stick with one topic. I think about my topic before I write, and I share my writing in a writing group. That is something I did not like to do at first, but now I do. I think my writing has a lot more voice now. Voice is the part of your writing that shows how you feel about your topic because the thoughts and feelings come from your heart. This year we read *Charlotte's Web*, and that is a book that I think has a lot of voice. I have also worked very hard on my word choice. I try to find just the right word to say what I mean and not just the first word that comes into my mind. The way I have grown the most is that I like to write a lot more than I use to, especially poems. I think I could be a poet if I wanted to, and I think my writing shows that.

Summary

1. Performance assessment can be used to improve student learning if you schedule practice events before the graded event.

2. Rubrics can be used to increase achievement by doing the following:

   - Help students understand the concepts of quality.

   - Provide meaningful feedback that fosters student improvement.

   - Offer students language for self-assessment.

   - Point the way toward productive revision.

   - Help students notice, track, and report on their own growth.

chapter

$$[\ 7\ ]$$

Communicating with Parents about Rubrics

Parents are brought into the process, too. "On back-to-school nights, I ask parents to write. . . . You should see the fear on their faces. . . . They even ask me if I'm going to collect the writing or if I'm going to read it. I tell them, no, it's just for them. But I do ask them to think about how writing was assessed when they were kids. They remember this sea of red marks—so that's what a lot of them expect from me. I also ask them if they know what they're really good at as writers. A lot of them don't have a clue. Then I pass out copies of the Six-Trait Scoring Guide for Students—and it's like a whole world opens up. One dad asked me, 'Where was this when I was going to school?'"

x

—V. Spandel
Creating Writers: Through 6-Trait Writing Assessment and Instruction,
Boston: Allyn & Bacon, 2005, p. 242

Parents generally want to know three things about their children's education: *what* they will be learning, *how* the teacher will determine if the student has succeeded, and *what support* will be available if the student has difficulty. It is important that parents understand how using rubrics fits into this picture. They may not need to understand all the details about rubrics described in this book—what strong and weak ones look like, how to develop them, and what all the different types are—but there are key topics to share with parents, so that when they see their children working with rubrics, or when they see rubric scores instead of grades on some assignments, they understand what they mean and why you used them.

What Rubrics Are and When You Use Them

Before you launch into an explanation of rubrics, it is helpful to give parents a little assessment context. Briefly define the four assessment methods and give a few examples of learning targets suited to each. Here you can point out the differences between knowledge/fact learning targets and more complex targets—those calling for *use* of that knowledge; e.g., problem solving, performance skills, and the creation of products. Share one or more examples of learning targets that you will be assessing using performance assessment and let parents know that performance assessment is used to measure these targets when no other method will yield accurate results. (See Chappuis & Chappuis, 2002, for a more in-depth explanation of keys to quality assessment for a parent audience.)

Point out that a performance assessment has two parts—the task or assignment (what you ask students to do) and the rubric (a description of the features important in a quality performance or product). You will want to define the terms *rubric*, *criteria*, and *descriptors*, perhaps in the context of a situation in which they are already familiar with features of quality; by

Figure 7.1 Key Topics

The following are key topics to address when speaking with parents:

- What rubrics are and when we use them
- How using rubrics benefits learning
- How rubrics are used in the classroom
- How to interpret rubric scores
- How parents can use rubrics with their children

---

explaining what they expect in a clean bedroom, for example. Figure 7.2 shows what definitions of these terms can look like in this context.

As another example, you may wish to use the context of dining out at a restaurant. People often tip their server based on the quality of service provided, including features such as promptness of service, cleanliness of the table, and quality of the meal. These are the *criteria* on which the decision will be based. The *descriptors* would define what a server would do in each of the criteria to receive a generous tip, a moderate tip, or a small tip. These and other common experiences introduce parents to the structure of rubrics as well as to their usefulness. Rubrics are not a recent invention; they are simply the basis on which we make certain judgments, written down.

After introducing rubrics in a familiar context, you may wish to explain them in an academic context. You may use the following explanation of an oral presentation rubric as a framework, but you would want to base your discussion on whatever rubric you are actually planning to use:

- Ask parents to think about oral presentations. What contributes to an effective oral presentation? Accurate content? Content that is organized in a way that leads listeners from beginning to end? Few "ums" and "ahs"? Eye contact with the audience? Terminology that the audience understands? Use of pictures, graphs, or other visual aids to understanding, as needed?

- We look for all these attributes in an effective oral presentation. Such a list is the beginning of a rubric for an oral presentation. The rubric identifies keys to success. It clarifies not only the features that contribute to a great oral presentation, but also what oral presentations at the medium and weak levels look like.

- Distribute the rubric you intend to use. (For an example, see the *Oral Presentation Rubric* in Appendix C and in the *Rubric Sampler* on the CD.) Encourage parents to notice the connections between their own ideas and the features represented on your rubric. Assure them that you will be teaching their offspring to progress through these levels of quality throughout the year.

Figure 7.2 Terms to Define for Parents

Definitions

Rubric: A list of features we consider important in a quality performance, experience, or product

Criteria: The specific features on the list

Descriptors: The words and phrases we use to explain what those features should and shouldn't look like

Example

A **rubric** for a clean bedroom lists what you expect to see. The **criteria** might be *Floor Is in Good Shape*, *Bed Is Made*, and *Clothes Are Put Away*. The **descriptors** for *Floor Is in Good Shape* might be, "Floor is completely picked up, with no trash, toys, food, dishes, bottles, cans, or clothes lying around. Floor is vacuumed, including under furniture."

How Using Rubrics Benefits Learning

Every one of us has been in the position of receiving a grade on a paper, a project, or a presentation and having no idea why we got that grade, what we should do differently next time to make the grade better, or what to continue doing next time to maintain a good grade. You can use this common experience to help parents understand the value both of defining precisely the characteristics of work that contribute to quality and of sharing them with students.

In most parents' own student careers, assessments will have been used primarily to assign grades. Parents should know that assessments can also help students learn at higher levels *before* they are graded. You can differentiate between these two purposes by labeling (1) the use of assessment information to determine grades as assessment *of* learning and (2) the use of assessment information to help students learn as assessment *for* learning.

To help parents understand the importance of assessment *for* learning, you can use an analogy such as this: A basketball coach doesn't just throw kids into a game without practice. During practice, the coach observes how well players perform certain skills and uses that information to help them practice and improve. This is assessment *for* learning; the coach is not using assessment information to give a grade; rather, the coach is using assessment information to help students maximize their performance before the next game.

You can then relate this idea back to the classroom. Invite parents to think about academic expectations such as writing, giving an oral presentation, speaking a foreign language, solving math problems, or planning scientific experiments. Using assessment to support and increase learning, you would teach to the expectations, observe students as they practice, and provide suggestions for improvement for some period of time (assessment *for* learning) before the next graded event (assessment *of* learning). Your goal would be to increase student achievement between the times when status information is reported to parents and others.

You may wish to share the following list of benefits that accrue for students, teachers, and parents when rubrics are used as assessments *for* learning:

- Students learn more quickly what it takes to produce a high-quality performance or product.

- Students develop the ability to self-assess—to identify what they are doing well and what they need to work on.

- Parents can gain insight into their children's strengths and the next steps in their learning.

- Teachers have better information to guide the next steps in instruction.

- Teachers can give feedback to students that describes exactly what they are doing well and what they need to tackle next.

How Rubrics Are Used in the Classroom

Parents want to know what to expect their children's learning to look like. You will want to highlight your strategies for teaching the elements of quality represented in your rubric, along with a brief rationale for each. You may wish to adapt the following list of instructional uses (described in Chapter 6) to your own context:

- *Before students are introduced to the rubric, they share what they already know about quality in the skill or product you are focusing on.* Students understand new information more readily if they first reflect on their own ideas before being asked to think about the ideas of others.

- *Students use the rubric to practice judging the quality of anonymous work.* When teachers select samples to represent specific strengths students are to work on and to highlight weaknesses to avoid, students deepen their understanding of what is expected before having to create the performance or product for a grade.

- *Some assignments come home marked with descriptions of strengths and areas for improvement, rather than grades. The wording reflects the concepts in the rubric.* Achievement improves at a greater rate when students have opportunities to practice with feedback and then are given time to act on that feedback before they submit work for a grade.

- *Students use the rubric to judge the quality of their own work: they identify areas where they are doing well and set goals for improvement where needed.* When students self-assess, ownership of their own learning increases and they are better equipped to take steps to improve.

- *Comments and grades on work may focus on one or two features of quality rather than all features represented on the rubric.* When learning how to complete a high-quality performance or product, students benefit from being able to focus on one part at a time rather than trying to learn how to do everything at once.

- *Students have opportunities to track their achievement and share their progress with parents.* Students' motivation to continue learning increases when they become aware of their own growth and track their improvement over time.

How to Interpret Rubric Scores

Most parents receive information about their child's progress from grades on assignments. However, when you are using rubrics to provide students with feedback before assigning a grade, the work may come home with only a set of descriptors of quality, or it may have only a rubric score on it. In these situations, you are using assessment to provide students with information about how to improve, which a grade does not accomplish. The work is still evaluated, but the results are to be acted on by either the teacher or the student, or both.

If you will be marking student work with the number or the word that matches a score point for a rubric, you will want to explain what the labels mean. (We will call these level labels *scores*.) It is also useful to explain that level labels are shorthand for the description of that level of work. This shorthand makes no sense without the descriptions that flesh out each label. If you can, share anonymous samples to illustrate levels of quality—this makes the meaning of each level designation even clearer.

Parents need to know that such changes in grading practices do not indicate less rigor or lower achievement. Assessment *for* learning practices do not alter the performance standards (how good is good enough)—they are just as rigorous, and they in fact bring about higher achievement—more students will achieve at desired levels. To reinforce this point, share your grading plan and summarize how you will convert rubric scores to grades. This is important and reassuring information, but a little goes a long way, so be sure your explanation is clear and short.

Remember that different rubrics from different content areas or different assessments may use totally different labels for the various score points. Many parents get frustrated by the language associated with the score points on a rubric—*proficient, emerging, exceeds mastery*, and so on. It can sound like jargon, and so we recommend that when talking to parents use straightforward language or use score points as the level labels. If you do use words or phrases, try to establish consistency across subjects and grade levels. It can be very confusing to parents when every rubric they see has different labels.

How Parents Can Use Rubrics with Their Children

When parents and children communicate about the child's achievement, they strengthen and reinforce that learning. What would you like parents to do with the information they receive from rubrics? Following are a few sample suggestions you may make to parents:

- Ask your child to explain what the rubric means in his own words.

- Ask your child to explain what a score on her work means.

- Ask your child what the score means he is good at and what it means he needs to improve.

- Ask your child to identify a part of her work that she thinks is strong or that needs work. Ask her to find the words in the rubric that describe the features of the part she identified.

- Work with your child to make a plan for revising the work based on the description of quality linked to the score he received.

Suggestions for Sharing Information with Parents

Up to this point in the chapter, we've looked at what is important for parents to know about the use of rubrics in the classroom. *When* and *how* you communicate this information is also important to consider.

When

For most parents, the more they know about their children's schools and classrooms, the more supportive they are of the education the students are receiving. In short, the closer parents get to schools the more they like them and approve of their work. This tells us that our communication with parents should not be limited to the traditional one-time open house or to similar events intended to convey lots of general information in a short period of time. Our communication with parents about what their students are experiencing in the classroom should be proactive and ongoing, in partnership with communication efforts from the school and the district.

The opening of the school year immediately sets the stage for introducing rubrics and preparing parents for their role in student assessment. If rubrics are used to evaluate any school, district, or state tests, give parents the criteria in advance when possible. This helps them understand what their children will be learning and how you will measure success. And if any high-stakes or other decisions are being made about students as a result of these tests, parents need to see how those decisions are made and how they may be justified.

How

The traditional formal and informal ways teachers share information with parents can also be effective for communicating about the use of rubrics. Monthly or weekly newsletters; back-to-school nights and open houses; e-bulletins to parents who have Internet access and e-mail addresses; and the day-to-day discussions you have with parents over the phone, over the backyard fence, and in the aisles of grocery stores all provide opportunities to help parents understand how you are using rubrics in your classroom. We would recommend that you plan how to use these opportunities; perhaps some general information goes out at back-to-school night, followed by district- or schoolwide newsletter articles. In your own communications with parents, you can then share specifics about how you will be using rubrics and which ones you will use.

Also consider the following ways to help parents learn:

- Create a monthly or quarterly newsletter dedicated to performance assessment. (This can be easier to do in partnership with other teachers.) Select one topic each issue and discuss it in some depth. Topics can include a description of what the phrases on the rubric mean, one trait at a time; the different types of rubrics (task specific vs. general, holistic vs. analytic); an explanation of the score point numbers or descriptors (*emerging, proficient*, etc.); the difference between marks (grades on individual pieces of work) and report card grades; how you will convert rubric score points to grades; what self-assessment activities your students will engage in and how they benefit learning; and other topics as described in this chapter and throughout this book.

- Give parents sample tasks with anonymous student work scored using your rubric. Then give them other samples to score on their own. After they have had a chance to try it themselves, as an option you may wish to share how you, the district, or the state would score the work.

- If there is a statewide rubric for the state accountability test, schedule a session to help them understand how your rubrics align to it.

- Identify opportunities for parents to give students feedback on a piece of work, using the language of the rubric. (This can even be an occasional homework assignment.)

Students' Role in Communicating with Parents

Finally and most importantly, remember the impact on learning created when students explain what they know. Students can do the following:

- Compare a current piece of their work to the rubric in class, and then that evening show their parents why they came to that judgment.

- While participating in (or leading) a conference with parents, students can review the criteria of the rubric and select goals for future work or performance based on that criteria.

- Share a sample of their work with parents and then reflect on their learning with ideas such as, "If I did this over I would . . . ," or "The best thing I did in this piece of work is . . . ," using the language of the rubric. This too can be homework.

- Show parents a learning log in which they have kept track of their progress. Students can explain their growth by referring to the criteria and the language of the rubric they are using to define *quality*.

Summary

1. Parents want to know what their children will be learning, how you will determine whether they have succeeded, and what support will be available for their children if they struggle. When you share information about rubrics, frame it in the context of these three main concerns.

2. To introduce rubrics to parents, briefly define the four assessment methods and then share the learning targets for which you will be using performance assessment.

3. Define *performance assessment, rubric, criteria,* and *descriptors* first within the context of everyday experiences and then in an academic context, with the rubric you will be using in your classroom.

4. To show how using rubrics benefits learning, differentiate between assessment *of* and *for* learning, first using experiences parents may have had and then with your classroom applications. Share benefits to students, parents, and teachers when rubrics are used instructionally.

5. Give examples of what instructional uses you will make of rubrics. Highlight strategies you will use to teach the elements of quality represented in your rubric.

6. Make sure parents understand the meaning of whatever symbols or words you will use when marking student work, and show how rubric scores will figure in the final grade. Be concise here.

7. Share suggestions for what parents can do with rubrics and rubric scores with their children to strengthen or reinforce the learning.

8. It is important to plan both when and how you will communicate about rubrics. The more parents know about their children's education, the more supportive they are. An ongoing approach to communication is more effective than a single, one-time event. Everyone benefits when students also participate in this communication—it *is* about them.

Glossary

Analytic rubric: A type of rubric that provides ratings of a performance or product along several different, important dimensions. The term is used primarily to describe one type of general rubric. Some people also use the term *analytical trait*. Contrast with *Holistic Rubric*.

Constructed response assessment: Assessments in which students provide their own, somewhat lengthy responses to a question or task. Constructed response assessments include extended written response (in which students write out a response to a performance task), performance assessment (in which students demonstrate a performance skill or create a product), and extended oral response.

Criteria: Important dimensions of student work that are defined separately in an analytic rubric. Sometimes also called *Traits*.

Descriptors: The numbered features under each *Indicator* in the *Rubric for Rubrics* and the numbered features under each criterion in the *Rubric for Tasks*. Also a term used more generally to denote what to look for in products or performances to help determine level of quality.

General rubric: A rubric designed so that it can be used across similar tasks. This contrasts with a *Task-Specific Rubric*, which can be used for a single task only. A general rubric is useful for constructed response tasks that focus on reasoning proficiency, performance skill, and product learning targets.

Holistic rubric: A type of rubric that results in a single, overall rating for an entire performance or product. The term is used primarily to describe one type of general rubric. Contrast with *Analytic Rubric*.

Indicators: Major subunits in the *Rubric for Rubrics* that help delineate what to look for in a classroom rubric to determine its level of quality. The *Rubric for Rubrics* has two criteria: *Coverage/Organization* and *Clarity*. *Coverage/Organization* has three indicators—*Content, Organization*, and *Number of Levels*. The criterion of *Clarity* has two indicators—*Levels Defined Well* and *Levels Parallel*. The term is also used more generally to denote what to look for in products and performances to help determine level of quality. In other contexts this term is used interchangeably with *descriptors*.

Learning targets: Statements of what teachers want students to know and be able to do. Also frequently called *content standards, benchmarks, indicators, goals, objectives*, and *intentions*. In this text, we define four types of learning targets: knowledge, reasoning, performance skills, and products that students create.

Logic rule: Our term for a process, partly formulaic and partly specific to the context, for converting rubric scores to grades.

Percentage equivalent: Our term for a rule that allows you to combine rubric scores with other forms of assessment results, yielding percentages to determine a final grade for a grading period.

Performance assessment: Assessment based on observation and judgment. One of several methods of assessment useful in the classroom. Particularly apt for assessing student reasoning proficiencies, performance skills, and products.

Performance task: The activity or exercise given to students to do, the results of which will be evaluated using a rubric. A performance task is one of two parts of a performance assessment, the other being the rubric.

Rubric: The written criteria by which a student product or performance will be judged. Good rubrics have levels defined using indicators and/or descriptors. A rubric is one of two parts of a performance assessment, the other being the performance task.

Scoring guide: A written set of statements that describe how student performance on a task will be evaluated. All rubrics are scoring guides, but not all scoring guides are rubrics. For example, task-specific scoring guides are not considered rubrics.

Selected response assessment: Assessment questions that are scored right/wrong. Students usually select a response from a list, such as with multiple-choice or matching items. We also include true-false and short answer items (one to several words) in this category. This is contrasted with *Constructed Response Assessment,* in which students provide their own, longer response to a question or task.

Targets: See *Learning Targets.*

Task-specific rubric: A scoring guide designed to be used with only a single task. This contrasts with a *General Rubric,* which can be used across similar tasks. Task-specific scoring is useful for constructed response questions that focus on student knowledge. Task-specific rubrics are also used when large numbers of responses must be scored quickly.

Traits: See *Criteria.*

Bibliography

General Bibliography

Arter, J. A. (2002). Rubrics, scoring guides, and performance criteria. In C. Boston (Ed.), *Understanding scoring rubrics* (pp. 14–24). College Park, MD: University of Maryland, ERIC Clearinghouse of Assessment & Evaluation.

Arter J. A., & McTighe, J. (2001). *Scoring rubrics in the classroom: Using performance criteria for assessing and improving student performance.* Thousand Oaks, CA: Corwin.

Assessment Reform Group. (1999). *Assessment for learning: Beyond the black box.* Cambridge, UK: University of Cambridge School of Education.

Babb, J. (2002). Finding the right words. In J. H. Shulman, A. Whittaker, & M. Lew (Eds.), *Using assessments to teach for understanding* (pp. 89–91). New York: Teachers College Press.

Bangert-Downs, R. L., Kulik, C-L. C., Kulik, J. A., & Morgan, M. T. (1991). The instructional effect of feedback in test-like events. *Review of Educational Research, 61*(2), 213–238.

Black, P., Harrison, C., Lee, C., Marshall, B., & Wiliam, D. (2002). *Working inside the black box: Assessment for learning in the classroom.* London: King's College Press.

Black, P., & Wiliam, D. (1998). Inside the black box: Raising standards through classroom assessment. *Phi Delta Kappan, 80*(2), 139–148.

Bloom, B. (1984). The search for methods of group instruction as effective as one to one tutoring. *Educational Leadership, 41*(8), 4–17.

Brookhart, S. M. (2004). *Grading.* Upper Saddle River, NJ: Merrill/Prentice Hall.

Brown, A. (1994). The advancement of learning. *Educational Researcher, 23*(8), 4–12.

Butler, R. (1988). Enhancing and undermining intrinsic motivation: The effects of task-involving and ego-involving evaluation on interest and performance. *British Journal of Educational Psychology, 58*, 1–14.

Butler, R., & Neuman, O. (1995). Effects of task and ego-achieving goals on help-seeking behaviours and attitudes. *Journal of Educational Psychology, 87*(2), 261–271.

Caine, R. N., & Caine, G. (1997). *Education on the edge of possibility.* Alexandria, VA: Association for Supervision & Curriculum Development.

Cameron, J., & Pierce, D. P. (1994). Reinforcement, reward, and intrinsic motivation: A meta-analysis. *Review of Educational Research, 64*(3), 363–423.

Chicago Public Schools (n.d.). How to create a rubric from scratch. Retrieved 9 November 2005 from http://www.intranet.cps.k12.il.us/Assessments/Ideas_and_Rubrics/Create_Rubric/

Clarke, S. (2001). *Unlocking formative assessment.* London, UK: Hodder & Stoughton.

Central Kitsap School District. (1999). *Physical education essential learnings.* Silverdale, WA: Author.

Central Kitsap School District. (2000a). *Grades K–6 language essential learnings.* Silverdale, WA: Author.

Central Kitsap School District. (2000b). *Grades 7–10 language essential learnings.* Silverdale, WA: Author.

Central Kitsap School District. (2001a). *Grades K–6 mathematics essential learnings.* Silverdale, WA: Author.

Central Kitsap School District. (2001b). *Science essential learnings.* Silverdale, WA: Author.

Central Kitsap School District. (2001c). *Social studies essential learnings.* Silverdale, WA: Author.

Central Kitsap School District. (2001d). *The student-friendly guide to mathematics problem solving.* Silverdale, WA: Author.

Chappuis, J., & Chappuis, S. (2002). *Understanding school assessment: A parent and community guide to helping students learn.* Portland, OR: Assessment Training Institute.

Chappuis, S., Stiggins, R. J., Arter, J., & Chappuis, J. (2004). *Assessment FOR learning: An action guide for school leaders.* Portland, OR: Assessment Training Institute.

Cicmanec, K. M., Johanson, G., & Howley, A. (2001, April). *High school mathematics teachers: Grading practice and pupil control ideology.* Paper presented at the American Educational Research Association annual meeting, Seattle, WA.

Danielson, C. (1997). *A collection of performance tasks and rubrics: Middle school mathematics.* Larchmont, NY: Eye on Education.

Dweck, C. S. (2001). *Self-theories: Their role in motivation, personality, and development.* Philadelphia: Psychology Press.

Ehrenberg, R. E., Brewer, D. J., Gamoran, A., & Willms, J. D. (2001). Does class size matter? *Scientific American, 285*(5), 78–85.

Fiderer, A. (1998). *35 rubrics and checklists to assess reading and writing.* New York: Scholastic.

Graves, D. (1983). *Writing: Teachers & children at work.* Portsmouth, NH: Heinemann.

Gregory, K., Cameron, C., & Davies, A. (2000). *Self-assessment and goal-setting.* Merville, BC: Connections.

Gregory, K., Cameron, C., & Davies, A. (2001). *Conferencing and reporting.* Merville, BC: Connections.

Guskey, T. R. (Ed.). (1996). *Communicating student learning.* Alexandria, VA: Association for Supervision & Curriculum Development.

Guskey, T. R. (2004). *The communication challenge of standards-based reporting.* N.P.

Guskey, T. R., & Bailey, J. (2001). *Developing grading and reporting systems for student learning.* Thousand Oaks, CA: Corwin.

Hattie, J., & Timperley, H. (2005, September). *The power of feedback.* Paper presented at the Second International Conference on Classroom Assessment, Portland, OR.

Herman, J. L., Baker, E. L., & Linn, R. L. (2004). Accountability systems in support of student learning: Moving to the next generation. *CRESST Line* (Spring), 1–7.

Hillocks, G. (1986). *Research on written composition: New directions for teaching.* Fairfax, VA: National Council of Teachers of English. (ERIC Document Retrieval Service No. ED265552)

Jensen, E. (1998). *Teaching with the brain in mind.* Alexandria, VA: Association for Supervision & Curriculum Development.

Johnson, B. (1996). *The performance assessment handbook: Performances & exhibitions.* Princeton, NJ: Eye on Education.

Kluger, A. N., & deNisi, A. (1996). The effects of feedback interventions on performance: A historical review, a meta-analysis, and a preliminary feedback intervention theory. *Psychological Bulletin, 119*(2), 254–284.

Lucas, C. (1992). Introduction: Writing portfolios—changes and challenges. In K. Yancey (Ed.), *Portfolios in the writing classroom* (pp. 1–11). Reston, VA: National Council of Teachers of English.

Matsumura, L. C., Pascal, J., Steinberg, J. R., & Valdez, R. (2002). *Classroom assignment scoring manual: Elementary school.* Los Angeles, CA: National Center for Research on Evaluation Standards & Student Testing, UCLA.

McMillan, J. H. (2001). Secondary teachers' classroom assessment and grading practices. *Educational Measurement: Issues & Practice, 20*(1), 20–32.

McTighe, J., & Wiggins, G. (1999). *The understanding by design handbook.* Alexandria, VA: Association for Supervision & Curriculum Development.

Mertler, C. A. (2001). Designing scoring rubrics for your classroom. *Practical Assessment, Research & Evaluation, 7*(25), n.p. Retrieved 4 August 2005 from http://PAREonline.net/getvn.asp?v=7&n=25

Mertler, C. A. (2002). Designing scoring rubrics for your classroom. In C. Boston (Ed.), *Understanding scoring rubrics: A guide for teachers* (pp. 72–81). College Park, MD: ERIC Clearinghouse on Assessment and Evaluation.

Moskal, B. M. (2000). Scoring rubrics: What, when and how? *Practical Assessment, Research & Evaluation, 7*(3), n.p. Retrieved 4 August 2005 from http://PAREonline.net/getvn.asp?v=7&n=3

Moskal, B. M., & Leydens, J. A. (2002). Scoring rubric development: Validity and reliability. In C. Boston (Ed.), *Understanding scoring rubrics: A guide for teachers* (pp. 25–33). College Park, MD: ERIC Clearinghouse on Assessment and Evaluation.

National Council of Teachers of Mathematics. (2003). *Mathematics assessment: A practical handbook.* Reston, VA: Author.

National Research Council. (1996). *National science education standards.* Washington, DC: National Academy Press.

North Thurston Public Schools. (2001). *K–12 arts curriculum.* Lacey, WA: Author.

O'Connor, K. (2002). *How to grade for learning: Linking grades to standards* (2nd ed.). Arlington Heights, IL: Skylight.

O'Sullivan, R., Arter, J., Hudson, M., Orsini, M., Stiggins, R. J., & Iovacchini, L. (2005). *Investigating the classroom assessment literacy of NBPTS board-certified teachers: Final report for policy makers.* Portland, OR: Assessment Training Institute.

Office of Educational Research & Improvement. (1997). *Studies of educational reform: Assessment of student performance.* Washington. DC: Author.

Office of Superintendent of Public Instruction. (2004a). *Washington state essential academic learning requirements: Arts.* Olympia, WA: Author. Retrieved 14 May 2004 from http://www.k12.wa.us/CurriculumInstruct/Arts/default.aspx

Office of Superintendent of Public Instruction. (2004b). *Washington state essential academic learning requirements: Civics.* Olympia, WA: Author. Retrieved 14 May 2004 from http://www.k12.wa.us/CurriculumInstruct/SocStudies/civicsEALRs.aspx

Office of Superintendent of Public Instruction. (2004c). *Washington state essential academic learning requirements: Social studies skills.* Olympia, WA: Author. Retrieved 14 May 2004 from http://www.k12.wa.us/CurriculumInstruct/SocStudies/socstudiesskillsEALRs.aspx

Park, C. S., Lane, S., Silver, E. A., & Magone, M. (2003). *Using assessment to improve middle-grades mathematics teaching and learning.* Reston, VA: National Council of Teachers of Mathematics.

Perlman, C. L. (2004). Performance assessment: Designing appropriate performance tasks and scoring rubrics. In J. E. Wall & G. R. Walz (Eds.), *Measuring up: Assessment issues for teachers, counselors, and administrators* (pp. 497–506). Greensboro, NC: CAPS Press.

Popham, W. J. (2000). *Modern educational measurement: Practical guidelines for educational leaders.* Boston: Allyn & Bacon.

Popham, W. J. (2002). *Classroom assessment: What teachers need to know.* Boston: Allyn & Bacon.

Regional Educational Laboratories. (1998). *Improving classroom assessment: A toolkit for professional developers*. Portland, OR: Northwest Regional Educational Laboratory. Retrieved 9 November 2005 from http://www.nwrel.org

Rohrmann, B. (2003). *Verbal qualifiers for rating scales: Sociolinguistic considerations and psychometric data*. University of Melbourne, Australia. Retrieved 26 October 2005 from www.psych.unimelb.edu.au/staff/rohrmann.html

Schmoker, M. (2002). The real causes of higher achievement. *SEDLetter, 14*(2), n.p. Retrieved 12 May 2004 from http://www.sedl.org/pubs/sedletter/v14n02/1.html

Schmoker, M., & Marzano, R. (1999). Realizing the promise of standards-based education. *Educational Leadership, 56*(6), 17–21. Retrieved 14 May 2004 from http://www.ascd.org/publications/ed_lead/199903/schmoker.html

Shavelson, R. J., Baxter, G. P., & Gao, X. (1993). Sampling variability of performance assessments. *Journal of Educational Measurement, 30*(3), 215–232.

Shavelson, R. J., Baxter, G. P., & Pine, J. (1992). Performance assessments: Political rhetoric and measurement reality. *Educational Researcher, 21*(4), 22–27.

Spandel, V. (2005). *Creating writers: Through 6-trait writing assessment and instruction*. Boston: Allyn & Bacon.

Stiggins, R. J. (2001). *Student-involved classroom assessment* (3rd ed). Upper Saddle River, NJ: Merrill/Prentice Hall.

Stiggins, R. J. (2005). *Student-involved assessment for learning* (4th ed.). Upper Saddle River, NJ: Merrill/Prentice Hall.

Stiggins, R. J., Arter, J. A., Chappuis, J., & Chappuis, S. (2004). *Classroom assessment* for *student learning: Doing it right—using it well*. Portland, OR: Assessment Training Institute.

Stiggins, R. J., & O'Connor, K. (2006). *A repair kit for grading: 15 fixes for broken grades*. Portland, OR: Educational Testing Service.

Tierney, R. J., Carter, M., & Desai, L. (1991). *Portfolio assessment in the reading-writing classroom*. Norwood, MA: Christopher-Gordon.

Tierney, R., & Simon, M. (2004). What's still wrong with rubrics: Focusing on the consistency of performance criteria across scale levels. *Practical Assessment, Research & Evaluation, 9*(2), n.p. Retrieved 4 August 2005 from http://PAREonline.net

Wiggins, G., & McTighe, J. (1998). *Understanding by design*. Alexandria, VA: Association for Supervision & Curriculum Development.

Bibliography: The Impact of Rubrics on Student Learning

Andrade, H. G. (1999a, April). *The role of instructional rubrics and self-assessment in learning to write: A smorgasbord of findings*. Paper presented at the American Educational Research Association annual meeting, Montreal. (ERIC Document Reproduction Service No. ED431029)

Andrade, H. G. (1999b, April). *Student self-assessment: At the intersection of metacognition and authentic assessment*. Paper presented at the American Educational Research Association annual meeting, Montreal. (ERIC Document Reproduction Service No. ED431030)

Arter, J. A., Spandel, V., Culham, R., & Pollard, J. (1994). *The impact of teaching students to be self-assessors of writing.* Paper presented at the American Educational Research Association annual meeting, San Francisco. (ERIC Document Reproduction Service No. ED370975)

Borko, H., Mayfield, V., & Marion, S. (1997). Teachers' developing ideas and practices about mathematics performance assessment: Successes, stumbling blocks, and implications for professional development. *Teaching & Teacher Education, 13*(3), 259–278.

Brookhart, S. M. (2005, April). *Research on formative classroom assessment.* Paper presented at the American Educational Research Association annual meeting, Montreal.

Carlson, J. I. (1997). *Objective self-evaluation of writing: Middle school students using Oregon's six-trait analytic writing scale to self-evaluate written work.* Master's thesis, Eastern Oregon University.

Clarke, D., & Stephens, M. (1995). The ripple effect: The instructional impact of the systemic introduction of performance assessment in mathematics. In M. Bierenbaum & F. Dochy (Eds.), *Evaluation in education and human services: Vol. 42. Alternatives in assessment of achievements, learning processes, and prior knowledge* (n.p.). Norwell, MA: Kluwer Academic.

Dean, C. (Ed.). (1995). *Assessment in action: Collaborative action research focused on mathematics and science assessments. Reports of twenty-three teacher-research projects.* Aurora, CO: Mid-Continent Regional Educational Laboratory. (ERIC Document Reproduction Service No. ED399170)

Edwins, S. D. (1995). *Increasing reflective writing and goal setting skills in high ability sixth-grade mathematics students.* Master's thesis, N.P. (ERIC Document Reproduction Service No. ED392065)

Gregait, L. H., Johnsen, D. R., & Nielsen, P. S. (1997). *Improving evaluation of student participation in physical education through self-assessment.* Master's thesis, Saint Xavier University, Chicago. (ERIC Document Reproduction Service No. ED415222)

Hillocks, G. (1986). *Research on written composition: New directions for teaching.* Fairfax, VA: National Council of Teachers of English. (ERIC Document Reproduction Service No. ED265552)

Klenowski, V. (1995). Student self-evaluation process in student-centered teaching and learning contexts of Australia and England. *Assessment in Education, 2,* 145–163.

Kowalewski, E., Murphy, J., & Starns, M. (2002). *Improving student writing in the elementary classroom.* Master's thesis, Saint Xavier University, Chicago. (ERIC Document Reproduction Service No. ED467516)

Ross, J. A., & Starling, M. (2005, April). *Effects of self-evaluation training on achievement and self-efficacy in a computer-supported learning environment.* Paper presented at the American Educational Research Association annual meeting, Montreal.

Shafer, W. D., Swanson, G., Bene, N., & Newberry, G. (1999, April). *Effects of teacher knowledge of rubrics on student achievement in four content areas.* Paper presented at the American Educational Research Association annual meeting, Montreal. (ERIC Document Reproduction Service No. ED430030)

Shepard, L. A. (2001, July). *Using assessment to help students think about learning.* Presentation at the Student-Involved Classroom Assessment conference, University of Colorado at Boulder.

Topping, K. (1998). Peer assessment between students in colleges and universities. *Review of Educational Research, 68*(3), 249–276.

White, B. Y., & Frederiksen, J. R. (1997). *The ThinkerTools Inquiry Project: Making scientific inquiry accessible to students.* ETS research report number MS-96-01. Retrieved 18 November 2005 from http://www.ets.org/research/researcher

Bibliography: The Impact of Assessment *for* Learning

Assessment Reform Group. (2002). *Testing, motivation and learning.* Cambridge, UK: University of Cambridge, Faculty of Education.

Black, P. (2003a, April). *Formative and summative assessment: Can they serve learning together?* Paper presented at the American Educational Research Association annual meeting, Chicago.

Black, P. (2003b, April). *The nature and value of formative assessment for learning.* Paper presented at the American Educational Research Association annual meeting, Chicago.

Black, P. (2003c, April). *A successful intervention—Why did it work?* Paper presented at the American Educational Research Association annual meeting, Chicago.

Black, P., Harrison, C., Lee, C., Marshall, B., & Wiliam, D. (2002). *Working inside the black box: Assessment for learning in the classroom.* London: King's College Press.

Black, P., & Wiliam, D. (1998). Inside the black box: Raising standards through classroom assessment. *Phi Delta Kappan, 80*(2), 139–148.

Bloom, B. (1984). The search for methods of group instruction as effective as one to one tutoring. *Educational Leadership, 41*(8), 4–17.

Brookhart, S. M. (2005, April). *Research on formative classroom assessment.* Paper presented at the American Educational Research Association annual meeting, Montreal.

Butler, R. (1988). Enhancing and undermining intrinsic motivation: The effects of task-involving and ego-involving evaluation on interest and performance. *British Journal of Educational Psychology, 58,* 1–14.

Dweck, C. (2001). *Self theories: Their role in personality, motivation and development.* Philadelphia: Psychology Press.

Gao, X. 1996). *Sampling variability and generalizability of Work Keys: Listening and writing scores.* ACT Research Report Series 996-1. Iowa City, IA: American College Testing.

Hattie, J. & Timperley, H. (2005, September). *The power of feedback.* Paper presented at the Second International Conference on Classroom Assessment, Portland, OR.

Hillocks, G. (1986). *Research on written composition: New directions for teaching.* Fairfax, VA: National Council of Teachers of English. (ERIC Document Retrieval Service No. ED265552)

Hunkins, F. P. (1995). *Teaching thinking through effective questioning.* Norwood, MA: Christopher-Gordon.

Khattri, N., Reeve, A. L., & Adamson, R. J. (1997). *Assessment of student performance: Studies of assessment reform.* Washington DC: U.S. Office of Education, Office of Educational Research & Improvement.

Knight, S. (2000). *Questions: Assessing and developing children's understanding and thinking in literacy.* Manchester, UK: Manchester School Improvement Service. Retrieved 2005 from http://www.aaia.org.uk

Meisels, S., Atkins-Burnett, S., Xue, Y., Bickel, D. D., & Son, S. H. (2003). Creating a system of accountability: The impact of instructional assessment on elementary children's achievement test scores. *Educational Policy Analysis Archives, 11*(9), n.p. Retrieved 15 March 2005 from http://epaa.asu.edu/epaa/v11n9/

Mendel, S. (n.d.). *Creating portraits of performance.* Aurora, CO: Peakview Elementary School.

Robinson, J. (2005, April). *Teachers' use of formative assessment in meeting the needs of targeted NCLB students.* Paper presented at the American Educational Research Association annual meeting, Montreal.

Rodriguiz, M. C. (2004). The role of classroom assessment in student performance on TIMMS. *Applied Measurement in Education, 17*(1), 1–24.

Sadler, D. R. (1989). Formative assessment and the design of instructional systems. *Instructional Science, 18*, 119–144.

Wiliam, D., & Lee, C. (2001, September). *Teachers developing assessments for learning: Impact on student achievement.* Paper presented at the 27th annual conference of the British Educational Research Association, University of Leeds, UK.

appendix

Rubric for Rubrics

Overview

The *Rubric for Rubrics* is a rubric for evaluating the quality of performance assessment rating scales, which we call *rubrics* or *scoring guides*. It describes the features of a rubric that make it useful for assessment and learning in the classroom. It is intended to be used with general, not task-specific rubrics.

We developed the *Rubric for Rubrics* to evaluate rubrics for use in the classroom, not for use with large-scale assessments such as state or provincial assessments. Although many features of quality would be the same for both uses, large-scale rubrics often end up with features that would be counterproductive in a rubric intended for classroom use. For example, developers of rubrics for large-scale uses frequently emphasize a quick, overall picture of student performance—no detail. Rubrics used in the classroom, on the other hand, often need to provide detailed diagnostic information to inform day-to-day instructional decisions.

Definitions:

- A *criterion* is a key dimension of quality useful to consider separately. The *Rubric for Rubrics* has two criteria: *Coverage/Organization* and *Clarity*.

- Subheads under each criterion are *indicators*, and the following numbered items are *descriptors*. An indicator, for example is, "Covers the right content." A descriptor for that indicator is, "The content of the rubric represents the best thinking in the field . . ." There are three indicators for the first criterion and two for the second criterion.

- *Levels* are points on a rating scale defining degrees of quality. There are typically three to six levels of performance on rubrics. The *Rubric for Rubrics* has five levels, ranging from *Strong* to *Weak.*

Content of the *Rubric for Rubrics*

Criterion 1: *Coverage/Organization*

The *content* of a classroom rubric defines what to look for in a student's product or performance to determine its quality; what will "count." Teachers and students use this content to determine what they must do in order to succeed. What students see is what you'll get. If the rubric has problems on this criterion, there is no need to continue to the *Clarity* criterion. There are three indicators for the first criterion.

Indicator 1A: Covers the Right Content

A classroom rubric should (1) bear a direct relationship to the content standards and learning targets it is intended to measure, (2) cover all essential features that create quality in a product or performance, (3) leave out all trivial or unrelated features, and (4) support and extend your understanding about what you actually *do* look for when evaluating student work.

Indicator 1B: Criteria Are Well Organized

The list of features that describe quality should be as concise as possible and organized into a usable form. This often involves identifying and grouping similar features into criteria and being sure that the relative importance given to each criterion represents its relative contribution to the quality of the product or performance as a whole.

Indicator I C: Number of Levels Fits Targets and Uses

The number of levels needs to be appropriate for the intended learning target and your use of the rubric. There needs to be enough levels to track student progress without so many that users can't distinguish among them.

Criterion 2: *Clarity*

A classroom rubric is *clear* to the extent that teachers, students, and others are likely to interpret the statements and terms in the rubric the same way. A rubric can be strong on the criterion of *Coverage/Organization* but weak on the criterion of *Clarity*—the rubric seems to cover the important dimensions of performance, but doesn't describe them very well. Likewise, a rubric can be strong on the criterion of *Clarity*, but weak on the criterion of *Coverage/Organization*—it's very clear what the rubric means, but it is not focused on the right criteria. There are two indicators for the criterion of *Clarity*.

Indicator 2A: Levels Defined Well

The key with *Clarity* is to define levels so transparently that students (and teachers) can see precisely what features of work cause people to agree that work is Strong, Medium, or Weak. The instructional usefulness of any rubric depends on the clarity of level descriptions.

Indicator 2B: Levels Parallel

Rubrics should include a parallel feature of work on each level. For example, if you find that a rubric for playing the violin contains "lackadaisical bowing" as one descriptor of a middle-level performance, then a statement about the quality of the bowing must be included at the Strong and Weak levels as well. If this descriptor is not referred to at other levels, the levels are not parallel.

How to Use the Rubric

The descriptors under each indicator are not meant to function as a checklist. Rather, they are meant to help users determine the level of quality of the classroom rubric under consideration. Not everything has to be present (or missing) for the classroom rubric to be judged to be at a particular level of quality. Ask yourself, "Which level of descriptors best describes the classroom rubric I'm considering?"

An odd number of levels is used because the middle level represents a balance of strengths and weaknesses. It would take some work to make it usable, but it probably is worth the effort. A Strong score doesn't necessarily mean that the classroom rubric under consideration is perfect; rather, it means that it would require very little work to get it ready for use. A Weak score means that the classroom rubric needs so much work that it probably isn't worth the effort—it's time to find another one. It might even be easier to begin from scratch.

Additionally, a Medium score does not mean *average*. This is a criterion-referenced scale, not a norm-referenced one. It is meant to describe levels of quality in a classroom rubric, not to compare those currently available. It could be that the typical currently available classroom rubric is closer to Weak than to Medium.

Although three levels are defined, it is in fact a *five-level* scale. Think of level 4 as a combination of characteristics from levels 5 and 3. Likewise, level 2 combines characteristics from levels 3 and 1.

Rubric for Rubrics

Criterion 1: COVERAGE/ORGANIZATION

A. Covers the Right Content

5—Strong	3—Medium	1—Weak
1. The content of the rubric represents the best thinking in the field about what it means to perform well on the skill or product under consideration.	1. Much of the content represents the best thinking in the field, but there are a few places that are questionable.	1. You can't tell what learning target(s) the rubric is intended to assess, or you can guess at the learning targets, but they don't seem important, or content is far removed from current best thinking in the field about what it means to perform well on the skill or product under consideration.
2. The content of the rubric aligns directly with the content standards/ learning targets it is intended to assess.	2. Some features don't align well with the content standards/learning targets it is intended to assess.	2. The rubric doesn't seem to align with the content standards/learning targets it is intended to assess.
3. The content has the "ring of truth"—your experience as a teacher confirms that the content is truly what you do look for when you evaluate the quality of a student performance or product. In fact, the rubric is insightful; it helps you organize your own thinking about what it means to perform well.	3. Much of the content is relevant, but you can easily think of some important things that have been left out or that have been given short shrift, or it contains an irrelevant criterion or descriptor that might lead to an incorrect conclusion about the quality of student performance.	3. You can think of many important dimensions of a quality performance or product that are not in the rubric, or content focuses on irrelevant features. You find yourself asking, "Why assess this?" or "Why should this count?" or "Why should students have to do it this way?"

Rubric for Rubrics (Continued)

Criterion 1: COVERAGE/ORGANIZATION (Continued)

B. Criteria are Well Organized

5—Strong	3—Medium	1—Weak
1. The rubric is divided into easily understandable criteria as needed. The number of criteria reflects the complexity of the learning target. If a holistic rubric is used, it's because a single criterion adequately describes performance.	1. The number of criteria needs to be adjusted a little: either a single criterion should be made into two criteria, or two criteria should be combined.	1. The rubric is holistic when an analytic one is better suited to the intended use or learning targets to be assessed; or the rubric is an endless list of everything; there is no organization; the rubric looks like a brainstormed list.
2. The details that are used to describe a criterion go together; you can see how they are facets of the same criterion.	2. Some details that are used to describe a criterion are in the wrong criterion, but most are placed correctly.	2. The rubric seems "mixed up"—descriptors that go together don't seem to be placed together. Things that are different are put together.
3. The relative emphasis on various features of performance is right—things that are more important are stressed more; things that are less important are stressed less.	3. The emphasis on some criteria or descriptors is either too small or too great; others are all right.	3. The rubric is out of balance—features of more importance are emphasized the same as features of less importance.
4. The criteria are independent. Each important feature that contributes to quality work appears in only one place in the rubric.	4. Although there are instances when the same feature is included in more than one criterion, the criteria structure holds up pretty well.	4. Descriptors of quality work are represented redundantly in more than one criterion to the extent that the criteria are really not covering different things.

C. Number of Levels Fits Targets and Uses

5—Strong	3—Medium	1—Weak
1. The number of levels of quality used in the rating scale makes sense. There are enough levels to be able to show student progress, but not so many levels that it is impossible to distinguish among them.	1. Teachers might find it useful to create more levels to make finer distinctions in student progress, or to merge levels to suit the rubric's intended use. The number of levels could be adjusted easily.	1. The number of levels is not appropriate for the learning target being assessed or intended use. There are so many levels it is impossible to reliably distinguish between them, or too few to make important distinctions. It would take major work to fix the problem.

Rubric for Rubrics (*Continued*)

Criterion 2: CLARITY

A. Levels Defined Well

5—Strong	3—Medium	1—Weak
1. Each score point (level) is defined with indicators and/or descriptors. *A plus:* There are examples of student work that illustrate each level of each trait.	1. Only the top level is defined. The other levels are not defined.	1. No levels are defined; the rubric is little more that a list of categories to rate followed by a rating scale.
2. There is enough descriptive detail in the form of concrete indicators, adjectives, and descriptive phrases that allow you to match a student performance to the "right" score. *A plus:* If students are to use the rubric, there are student-friendly versions, and/or versions in foreign languages for ELL students.	2. There is some attempt to define terms and include descriptors, but some key ideas are fuzzy in meaning.	2. Wording of the levels, if present, is vague or confusing. You find yourself saying such things as, "I'm confused," or "I don't have any idea what this means." Or, the only way to distinguish levels is with words such as *extremely, very, some, little,* and *none;* or *completely, substantially, fairly well, little,* and *not at all.*
3. Two independent users, with training and practice, assign the same rating most of the time. *A plus:* There is information on rater agreement rates that shows that raters can exactly agree on a score 65% of the time, and within one point 98% of the time.	3. You have a question whether independent raters, even with practice, could assign the same rating most of the time.	3. It is unlikely that independent raters could consistently rate work the same, even with practice.
4. If counting the number or frequency of something is included as an indicator; changes in such counts really are indicators of changes in quality.	4. There is some descriptive detail in the form of words, adjectives, and descriptive phrases, but counting the frequency of something or vague quantitative words are also present.	4. Rating is almost totally based on counting the number or frequency of something, even though quality is more important than quantity.
5. Wording is descriptive, not evaluative.	5. Wording is mostly descriptive of the work, but there are a few instances of evaluative labels.	5. Wording tends to be evaluative rather than descriptive of the work; e.g., work is "mediocre," "above average," or "clever."

Rubric for Rubrics (*Continued*)

Criterion 2: CLARITY (*Continued*)		
B. Levels Parallel		
5—Strong	*3—Medium*	*1—Weak*
1. The levels of the rubric are parallel in content—if an indicator of quality is discussed in one level, it is discussed in all levels. If the levels are not parallel, there is a good explanation why.	1. The levels are mostly parallel in content, but there are some places where there is an indicator at one level that is not present at the other levels.	1. Levels are not parallel in content and there is no explanation of why, or the explanation doesn't make sense.

Classroom Rubric Analysis Form

Rubric: _____

_____

Criterion	Indicator	Rating	Rationale (use words and phrases from the Rubric for Rubrics)
Coverage/ Organization	1A: Covers the Right Content		
	1B: Criteria Are Well Organized		
	1C: Number of Levels Fits Targets and Uses		
Clarity	2A: Levels Defined Well		
	2B: Levels Parallel		

appendix

[B]

Rubric Sampler Table of Contents

English Language Arts

1. Reading Developmental Continuum (Primary)
2. K–5 Developmental Writing Scale
3. 6 + 1 Trait™ Writing Assessment Scoring Guide (Grades 3–12)
4. Six-Trait Writing Rubric Student-Friendly Version (Grades 3–8)
5. Oral Presentation Rubric (Grades 4–12)

Mathematics

6. Comparing Parks (Grade 5)
7. Number Patterns (Grade 5)
8. Mathematical Problem Solving: A Three-Trait Model Adult Version (Grades 3–12)
9. Mathematical Problem-Solving: A Three-Trait Model Student-Friendly Version (Grades 3–4)

Music

10. Rubric for Music Composition (Grade 5)
11. Music Create (Grades 7–12)
12. Rubric for Critiquing Music (Grades 7–12)

Physical Education

13. My Fifth-Grade Movement Routine Self-Assessment

Science

14. K–2 Science Continuum

15. Exemplars Primary Science Rubric

16. General Science Rubric (Grades 3–8)

Social Studies

17. Battle of Normandy Poster (Grade 10)

18. Essay Scoring Criteria, Secondary Social Studies

General

19. Beginning Research Writing (Grade 1)

20. Criteria for Judging the Whole Portfolio (Grades 3–12)

21. Seminar Discussion Rubric (Grades 5–12)

22. General Conceptual Understanding Rubric (Grades 5–12)

23. Assessing "Intellectual Quality" of Student Work (Grades 5–12)

24. Technical Writing Rubric (Grades 5–12)

25. Research Paper Rubric (Grades 7–College)

26. Teaming Rubric (Grades 7–College)

appendix

[C]

Rubric Sampler Rubrics Referenced in the Text

Evaluations for the remaining rubrics in the Rubric Sampler
can be found at http://www.assessmentinst.com/rubrics.html

Criteria for Judging the Whole Portfolio (Grades 3–12)

Sometimes it is helpful to look at the story the whole portfolio tells—quite apart from the quality of individual pieces of work within that portfolio. The following criteria were developed to help you take the "whole story" approach to looking at a portfolio in any content area. You may wish to consider some or all of these criteria, depending on the purpose of the portfolio and what you and your students hold to be important. Are there other criteria that also influence your thinking about the strength or power of a portfolio? Please note them—and make them known to your students.

Change Over Time

Strong

The student selects material that clearly demonstrates growth in one or more specific areas. Examples might be math problem-solving skill or development of ideas in writing. In reviewing the examples, the reviewer can easily see how and in what areas the student has grown. The self-reflection (if present) generally matches what the reviewer sees.

Developing

The samples show evidence of some growth, but the growth is limited. That is, the change from one sample to another is evident but not dramatic. Self-reflection, if present, may comment on changes that are not immediately apparent to the reviewer in looking at the student's work.

Not Yet

The samples in the portfolio do not show evidence of noticeable student growth or change over time. Either noticeable growth has not occurred, or the student has not selected the samples of work that would illustrate that growth clearly.

Diversity

Strong

The portfolio clearly demonstrates that the student has tried a variety of tasks/projects/assignments/challenges. There is great variety in the kinds of work presented or the outcomes/skills demonstrated. For instance, a math portfolio might include some problem analysis, samples of graphing skill, a problem-solving task that shows more than one solution, good use of math terminology, and a project showing application of math skills.

Developing

The portfolio reflects some diversity. Tasks are not all parallel and do not all demonstrate identical outcomes. For instance, a math portfolio might include open-ended problem solving with analysis of how the student did the task together with samples showing correct application of math procedures, concepts or symbols.

Not Yet

The portfolio reflects minimal diversity. All tasks represented are more or less alike, and demonstrate the same outcomes/skills.

Evidence of Thinking

Strong

The work in the portfolio provides evidence that the student has identified, analyzed, planned strategies, and worked through the solution to a problem or question. For instance, a high school science student might tackle the question of how to preserve wetlands in a rapidly developing area. An elementary science student might consider the question of whether rats can thrive on a vegetarian diet.

Developing

The work in the portfolio shows some evidence of thinking, reasoning, analyzing or problem solving, but the student may not have worked all the way through a solution, or may have missed opportunities to pull together interesting conclusions or plot alternate strategies. Still, the student's work overall shows signs of planning and purposeful effort.

Not Yet

The student has not included in the portfolio any work that clearly demonstrates purposeful planning of strategies, problem solving, analysis of a situation, reasoning out a conclusion, or considering alternative solutions.

Self-Reflection

Strong

Several (or more) examples of self-reflection show thoughtful consideration of personal strengths and needs based on in-depth understanding of criteria. Reflections may also include a statement of personal goals; responses to learning, to a unit of study, or to an assignment; a summary of growth over time; or other insight regarding the personal, individual story this student's portfolio tells.

Developing

Self-reflections included within the portfolio provide at least a superficial analysis of strengths and needs, which may or may not be tied to specific criteria for judging performance or growth. The student may include comments on what he/she likes or dislikes about a content area or unit of study, or about what he/she finds difficult or challenging; but the reflections may not include insights regarding growth, needs, goals, or changes in performance or learning styles over time.

Not Yet
Either no self-reflection is included within the portfolio, or the self-reflection is rudimentary: e.g., "I put this in because I like it"; "I included this in my portfolio because it took me a long time to do it"; "This is in my portfolio because we were asked to put it in."

Structure and Organization

Strong

The student has formatted and arranged the portfolio in a way that invites the reader inside. Items within the portfolio are clearly labeled and dated; the sequence is purposeful. All or most of the following are included: a table of contents, a main title page or title pages for major sections, an introductory letter to reviewers, a statement of purpose (may be contained within the introductory letter), criteria or rating scales (if relevant), and a closing, summary comment, or reflection.

Developing

The portfolio is arranged and formatted in a way that enables the reader to make sense of it with a little work. Most items within the portfolio are labeled, dated or both. At least some of the following items are included: table of contents, letter of introduction, statement of purpose, title pages, criteria/rating scales, closing reflection.

Not Yet

Arrangement and formatting of the portfolio make it difficult for the reviewer to determine when and under what circumstances it was assembled. Few items (if any) are clearly labeled or dated. Most or all of the following are missing: table of contents, letter of introduction, statement of purpose, title pages, criteria/ rating scales, closing reflection.

6+1 Trait™ Writing Assessment Scoring Guide (Grades 3–12)

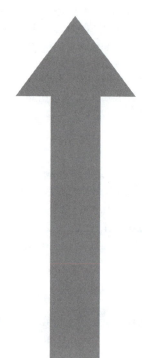

6+ 1 Trait™ Writing
Assessment Scoring Guide

Wow!
Exceeds expectations

5 Strong
Shows control and skill in this trait; many strengths present

4 Effective
On balance, the strengths outweigh the weaknesses; a small amount of revision is needed

3 Developing
Strengths and need for revision are about equal; about half-way home

2 Emerging
Need for revision outweighs strengths; isolated moments hint at what the writer has in mind

1 Not Yet
A bare beginning; writer not yet showing any control

6+1 Trait™ Writing

Ideas and Content (Development)

5   This paper is clear and focused. It holds the reader's attention. Relevant anecdotes and details enrich the central theme.

A. The topic is narrow and manageable.

B. Relevant, telling, quality details give the reader important information that goes beyond the obvious or predictable.

C. Reasonably accurate details are present to support the main ideas.

D. The writer seems to be writing from knowledge or experience; the ideas are fresh and original.

E. The reader's questions are anticipated and answered.

F. Insight—an understanding of life and a knack for picking out what is significant—is an indicator of high level performance, though not required.

3   The writer is beginning to define the topic, even though development is still basic or general.

A. The topic is fairly broad; however, you can see where the writer is headed.

B. Support is attempted, but doesn't go far enough yet in fleshing out the key issues or story line.

C. Ideas are reasonably clear, though they may not be detailed, personalized, accurate, or expanded enough to show in-depth understanding or a strong sense of purpose.

D. The writer seems to be drawing on knowledge or experience, but has difficulty going from general observations to specifics.

E. The reader is left with questions. More information is needed to "fill in the blanks."

F. The writer generally stays on the topic but does not develop a clear theme. The writer has not yet focused the topic past the obvious.

1 As yet, the paper has no clear sense of purpose or central theme. To extract meaning from the text, the reader must make inferences based on sketchy or missing details. The writing reflects more than one of these problems:

A. The writer is still in search of a topic, brainstorming, or has not yet decided what the main idea of the piece will be.

B. Information is limited or unclear or the length is not adequate for development.

C. The idea is a simple restatement of the topic or an answer to the question with little or no attention to detail.

D. The writer has not begun to define the topic in a meaningful, personal way.

E. Everything seems as important as everything else; the reader has a hard time sifting out what is important.

F. The text may be repetitious, or may read like a collection of disconnected, random thoughts with no discernable point.

Organization

5 The organization enhances and showcases the central idea or theme. The order, structure, or presentation of information is compelling and moves the reader through the text.

A. An inviting introduction draws the reader in; a satisfying conclusion leaves the reader with a sense of closure and resolution.

B. Thoughtful transitions clearly show how ideas connect.

C. Details seem to fit where they're placed; sequencing is logical and effective.

D. Pacing is well controlled; the writer knows when to slow down and elaborate, and when to pick up the pace and move on.

E. The title, if desired, is original and captures the central theme of the piece.

F. Organization flows so smoothly the reader hardly thinks about it; the choice of structure matches the purpose and audience.

3   The organizational structure is strong enough to move the reader through the text without too much confusion.

A. The paper has a recognizable introduction and conclusion. The introduction may not create a strong sense of anticipation; the conclusion may not tie-up all loose ends.

B. Transitions often work well; at other times, connections between ideas are fuzzy.

C. Sequencing shows some logic, but not under control enough that it consistently supports the ideas. In fact, sometimes it is so predictable and rehearsed that the structure takes attention away from the content.

D. Pacing is fairly well controlled, though the writer sometimes lunges ahead too quickly or spends too much time on details that do not matter.

E. A title (if desired) is present, although it may be uninspired or an obvious restatement of the prompt or topic.

F. The organization sometimes supports the main point or storyline; at other times, the reader feels an urge to slip in a transition or move things around.

1   The writing lacks a clear sense of direction. Ideas, details, or events seem strung together in a loose or random fashion; there is no identifiable internal structure. The writing reflects more than one of these problems:

A. There is no real lead to set-up what follows, no real conclusion to wrap things up.

B. Connections between ideas are confusing or not even present.

C. Sequencing needs lots and lots of work.

D. Pacing feels awkward; the writer slows to a crawl when the reader wants to get on with it, and vice versa.

E. No title is present (if requested) or, if present, does not match well with the content.

F. Problems with organization make it hard for the reader to get a grip on the main point or story line.

Voice

5 The writer speaks directly to the reader in a way that is individual, compelling and engaging. The writer crafts the writing with an awareness and respect for the audience and the purpose for writing.

A. The tone of the writing adds interest to the message and is appropriate for the purpose and audience.

B. The reader feels a strong interaction with the writer, sensing the person behind the words.

C. The writer takes a risk by revealing who he or she is consistently throughout the piece.

D. Expository or persuasive writing reflects a strong commitment to the topic by showing why the reader needs to know this and why he or she should care.

E. Narrative writing is honest, personal, and engaging and makes you think about, and react to, the author's ideas and point of view.

3 The writer seems sincere but not fully engaged or involved. The result is pleasant or even personable, but not compelling.

A. The writer seems aware of an audience but discards personal insights in favor of obvious generalities.

B. The writing communicates in an earnest, pleasing, yet safe manner.

C. Only one or two moments here or there intrigue, delight, or move the reader. These places may emerge strongly for a line or two, but quickly fade away.

D. Expository or persuasive writing lacks consistent engagement with the topic to build credibility.

E. Narrative writing is reasonably sincere, but doesn't reflect unique or individual perspective on the topic.

1 **The writer seems indifferent, uninvolved, or distanced from the topic and/or the audience. As a result, the paper reflects more than one of the following problems:**

A. The writer is not concerned with the audience. The writer's style is a complete mismatch for the intended reader or the writing is so short that little is accomplished beyond introducing the topic.

B. The writer speaks in a kind of monotone that flattens all potential highs or lows of the message.

C. The writing is humdrum and "risk-free."

D. The writing is lifeless or mechanical; depending on the topic, it may be overly technical or jargonistic.

E. The development of the topic is so limited that no point of view is present—zip, zero, zilch, nada.

Word Choice

5 **Words convey the intended message in a precise, interesting, and natural way. The words are powerful and engaging.**

A. Words are specific and accurate. It is easy to understand just what the writer means.

B. Striking words and phrases often catch the reader's eye and linger in the reader's mind.

C. Language and phrasing is natural, effective, and appropriate for the audience.

D. Lively verbs add energy while specific nouns and modifiers add depth.

E. Choices in language enhance the meaning and clarify understanding.

F. Precision is obvious. The writer has taken care to put just the right word or phrase in just the right spot.

3   The language is functional, even if it lacks much energy. It is easy to figure out the writer's meaning on a general level.

A. Words are adequate and correct in a general sense, and they support the meaning by not getting in the way.

B. Familiar words and phrases communicate but rarely capture the reader's imagination.

C. Attempts at colorful language show a willingness to stretch and grow but sometimes reach beyond the audience (thesaurus overload!).

D. Despite a few successes, the writing is marked by passive verbs, everyday nouns, and mundane modifiers.

E. The words and phrases are functional with only one or two fine moments.

F. The words may be refined in a couple of places, but the language looks more like the first thing that popped into the writer's mind.

1   The writer demonstrates a limited vocabulary or has not searched for words to convey specific meaning.

A. Words are so nonspecific and distracting that only a very limited meaning comes through.

B. Problems with language leave the reader wondering. Many of the words just don't work in this piece.

C. Audience has not been considered. Language is used incorrectly making the message secondary to the misfires with the words.

D. Limited vocabulary and/or misused parts of speech seriously impair understanding.

E. Words and phrases are so unimaginative and lifeless that they detract from the meaning.

F. Jargon or clichés distract or mislead. Redundancy may distract the reader.

Sentence Fluency

5   **The writing has an easy flow, rhythm, and cadence. Sentences are well built, with strong and varied structure that invites expressive oral reading.**

A. Sentences are constructed in a way that underscores and enhances the meaning.

B. Sentences vary in length as well as structure. Fragments, if used, add style. Dialogue, if present, sounds natural.

C. Purposeful and varied sentence beginnings add variety and energy.

D. The use of creative and appropriate connectives between sentences and thoughts shows how each relates to, and builds upon, the one before it.

E. The writing has cadence; the writer has thought about the sound of the words as well as the meaning. The first time you read it aloud is a breeze.

3   **The text hums along with a steady beat, but tends to be more pleasant or businesslike than musical, more mechanical than fluid.**

A. Although sentences may not seem artfully crafted or musical, they get the job done in a routine fashion.

B. Sentences are usually constructed correctly; they hang together; they are sound.

C. Sentence beginnings are not ALL alike; some variety is attempted.

D. The reader sometimes has to hunt for clues (e.g., connecting words and phrases like however, therefore, naturally, after a while, on the other hand, to be specific, for example, next, first of all, later, but as it turned out, although, etc.) that show how sentences interrelate.

E. Parts of the text invite expressive oral reading; others may be stiff, awkward, choppy, or gangly.

1 The reader has to practice quite a bit in order to give this paper a fair interpretive reading. The writing reflects more than one of the following problems:

A. Sentences are choppy, incomplete, rambling or awkward; they need work. Phrasing does not sound natural. The patterns may create a sing-song rhythm, or a chop-chop cadence that lulls the reader to sleep.

B. There is little to no "sentence sense" present. Even if this piece was flawlessly edited, the sentences would not hang together.

C. Many sentences begin the same way—and may follow the same patterns (e.g., subject-verb-object) in a monotonous pattern.

D. Endless connectives (and, and so, but then, because, and then, etc.) or a complete lack of connectives create a massive jumble of language.

E. The text does not invite expressive oral reading.

Conventions

5 The writer demonstrates a good grasp of standard writing conventions (e.g., spelling, punctuation, capitalization, grammar, usage, paragraphing) and uses conventions effectively to enhance readability. Errors tend to be so few that just minor touch-ups would get this piece ready to publish.

A. Spelling is generally correct, even on more difficult words.

B. The punctuation is accurate, even creative, and guides the reader through the text.

C. A thorough understanding and consistent application of capitalization skills are present.

D. Grammar and usage are correct and contribute to clarity and style.

E. Paragraphing tends to be sound and reinforces the organizational structure.

F. The writer may manipulate conventions for stylistic effect— and it works! The piece is very close to being ready to publish.

Grades 7 and Up Only: The writing is sufficiently complex to allow the writer to show skill in using a wide range of conventions. For writers at younger ages, the writing shows control over those conventions that are grade/age appropriate.

3 The writer shows reasonable control over a limited range of standard writing conventions. Conventions are sometimes handled well and enhance readability; at other times, errors are distracting and impair readability.

A. Spelling is usually correct or reasonably phonetic on common words, but more difficult words are problematic.

B. End punctuation is usually correct; internal punctuation (commas, apostrophes, semicolons, dashes, colons, parentheses) is sometimes missing/wrong.

C. Most words are capitalized correctly; control over more sophisticated capitalization skills may be spotty.

D. Problems with grammar or usage are not serious enough to distort meaning but may not be correct or accurately applied all of the time.

E. Paragraphing is attempted but may run together or begin in the wrong places.

F. Moderate editing (a little of this, a little of that) would be required to polish the text for publication.

1 Errors in spelling, punctuation, capitalization, usage, and grammar and/or paragraphing repeatedly distract the reader and make the text difficult to read. The writing reflects more than one of these problems:

A. Spelling errors are frequent, even on common words.

B. Punctuation (including terminal punctuation) is often missing or incorrect.

C. Capitalization is random and only the easiest rules show awareness of correct use.

D. Errors in grammar or usage are very noticeable, frequent, and affect meaning.

E. Paragraphing is missing, irregular, or so frequent (every sentence) that it has no relationship to the organizational structure of the text.

F. The reader must read once to decode, then again for meaning. Extensive editing (virtually every line) would be required to polish the text for publication.

Presentation—Optional

5   The form and presentation of the text enhances the ability for the reader to understand and connect with the message. It is pleasing to the eye.

A. If handwritten (either cursive or printed), the slant is consistent, letters are clearly formed, spacing is uniform between words, and the text is easy to read.

B. If word-processed, there is appropriate use of fonts and font sizes which invites the reader into the text.

C. The use of white space on the page (spacing, margins, etc.) allows the intended audience to easily focus on the text and message without distractions. There is just the right amount of balance of white space and text on the page. The formatting suits the purpose for writing.

D. The use of a title, side heads, page numbering, bullets, and evidence of correct use of a style sheet (when appropriate) makes it easy for the reader to access the desired information and text. These markers allow the hierarchy of information to be clear to the reader.

E. When appropriate to the purpose and audience, there is effective integration of text and illustrations, charts, graphs, maps, tables, etc. There is clear alignment between the text and visuals. The visuals support and clarify important information or key points made in the text.

3   The writer's message is understandable in this format.

A. Handwriting is readable, although there may be discrepancies in letter shape and form, slant, and spacing that may make some words or passages easier to read than others.

B. Experimentation with fonts and font sizes is successful in some places, but begins to get fussy and cluttered in others. The effect is not consistent throughout the text.

C. While margins may be present, some text may crowd the edges. Consistent spacing is applied, although a different choice may make text more accessible (e.g., single, double, or triple spacing).

D. Although some markers are present (titles, numbering, bullets, side heads, etc.), they are not used to their fullest potential as a guide for the reader to access the greatest meaning from the text.

E. An attempt is made to integrate visuals and the text although the connections may be limited.

1 The reader receives a garbled message due to problems relating to the presentation of the text.

A. Because the letters are irregularly slanted, formed inconsistently, or incorrectly, and the spacing is unbalanced or not even present, it is very difficult to read and understand the text.

B. The writer has gone wild with multiple fonts and font sizes. It is a major distraction to the reader.

C. The spacing is random and confusing to the reader. There may be little or no white space on the page.

D. Lack of markers (title, page numbering, bullets, side heads, etc.) leave the reader wondering how one section connects to another and why the text is organized in this manner on the page.

E. The visuals do not support or further illustrate key ideas presented in the text. They may be misleading, indecipherable, or too complex to be understood.

Mathematical Problem Solving: A Three-Trait Model, Adult Version (Grades 3–12)

Mathematical Concepts and Procedures

5 A strong performance occurs when the student demonstrates extensive understanding of the mathematical concepts and related procedures and uses them correctly. The student:

- Understands mathematical concepts and related procedures.
- Uses all necessary information from the problem.
- Performs computation(s) accurately or with only minor errors.

3 A developing performance occurs when the student demonstrates general understanding of the mathematical concepts and related procedures, but there may be some gaps or misapplication. The student:

- Partially understands mathematical concepts and related procedures.
- Uses some necessary information from the problem.
- May make some computational errors.

1 A weak performance occurs when the student demonstrates little or no understanding of mathematical concepts and related procedures. Application, if attempted, is incorrect. The student:

- Does not appear to understand mathematical concepts and related procedures.
- Does not use information from the problem or uses irrelevant information.
- Does no computation; or does computation that is unrelated to the problem.

Problem Solving

5 A strong performance occurs when the student selects or devises and uses an efficient, elegant, or sophisticated strategy to solve the problem.

- The student translates the problem into a useful mathematical form.
- The student applies the selected plan(s) or strategy(ies) through to completion; no pieces are missing.
- The plan or strategy may incorporate multiple approaches.
- Pictures, models, diagrams, and symbols, if used, enhance the strategy.
- The solution is reasonable and consistent with the context of the problem.

3 A developing performance occurs when the student selects or devises a plan or strategy, but it is partially unworkable.

- The student leaves gaps in framing or carrying out the strategy.
- The strategy may work in some parts of the problem, but not in others.
- The strategy is appropriate but incomplete in development or application.
- Results of computation, even if correct, may not fit the context of the problem.

1 A weak performance occurs when the student shows no evidence of a strategy or has attempted to use a completely inappropriate strategy.

- The student shows no attempt to frame the problem or translates the problem into an unrelated mathematical form.
- The strategy is inappropriate, misapplied, or disconnected.
- Pictures, models, diagrams, and symbols, if used, may bear some relationship to the problem.
- The solution is not reasonable and/or does not fit the context of the problem.

Mathematical Communication

5 A strong performance occurs when a student clearly explains in words, numbers, and/or diagrams the strategy used to solve the problem and the solution itself.

- The problem could be solved following the explanation. It is clearly explained and organized.
- The explanation is coherent and complete. There are no gaps in reasoning. Nothing is left out.
- The student presents logical arguments to justify strategy or solution.
- The explanations may include examples and/or counterexamples.
- Charts, pictures, symbols, and diagrams, when used, enhance the reader's understanding of what was done and why it was done.
- Few inferences are required to figure out what the student did and why.
- Correct mathematical language is used.

3 A developing performance occurs when the student's problem-solving process is partially explained, but requires some inferences in order to figure it out completely.

- The student attempts to use mathematical language, but may not have used all terms correctly.
- Some key elements are included in the explanation.
- The student explains the answer, but not the reasoning or explains the process, but not the solution.
- Charts, pictures, symbols, and diagrams, if used, provide some explanation of the major elements of the solution process.

1 A weak performance occurs when the student's explanation does not describe the process used or the solution to the problem.

- Charts, pictures, symbols, and diagrams, when used, interfere with the reader's understanding of what was done and why it was done.
- The explanation appears to be unrelated to the problem.
- The reader cannot follow the student's explanation.
- Little or no explanation of the thinking/reasoning is shown.
- The explanation only restates the problem.
- Many inferences are required to follow the student's work.
- Incorrect or misapplied mathematical language interferes with the reader's ability to understand the explanation.

General Science Rubric (Grades 3–8)

Level	Scientific Procedures and Reasoning	Strategies	Scientific Communication/ Using Data	Scientific Concepts and Related Content
Novice	Did not use appropriate scientific tools or technologies (e.g., rulers, pH paper, hand lens, computer, reference materials, etc.) to gather data (via measuring and observing).	No evidence of a strategy or procedure, or used a strategy that did not bring about successful completion of task investigation.	No explanation, or the explanation could not be understood, or was unrelated to the task investigation.	No use, or mostly inappropriate use, of scientific terminology.
		No evidence of scientific reasoning used.	Did not use, or inappropriately used scientific representations and notation (e.g., symbols, diagrams, graphs, tables, etc.).	No mention or inappropriate references to relevant scientific concepts, principles, or theories (big ideas).
		There were so many errors in the process of investigation that the task could not be completed.	No conclusions stated, or no data recorded.	Some evidence of understanding observable characteristics and properties or objects, organisms, and/or materials used.
Apprentice	Attempted to use appropriate tools and technologies (e.g., rules, pH papers, hand lens, computer, reference materials, etc.) to gather data (via measuring and observing) but some information was inaccurate or incomplete.	Used a strategy that was somewhat useful, leading to partial completion of the task/ investigation.	An incomplete explanation or explanation not clearly presented (e.g., out of sequence, missing step).	Used some relevant scientific terminology.
		Some evidence of scientific reasoning used.	Attempted to use appropriate scientific representations and notations, but were incomplete (e.g., no labels on chart).	Minimal reference to relevant scientific concepts, principles, or theories (big ideas).
		Attempted but could not completely carry out testing a question, recording all data, and stating conclusions.	Conclusions not supported or were only partly supported by data.	Evidence of understanding observable characteristics and properties of objects, organisms, and/or materials used.

Level	Scientific Procedures and Reasoning	Strategies	Scientific Communication/ Using Data	Scientific Concepts and Related Content
Practitioner	Effectively used some appropriate tools and technologies (e.g., rulers, pH paper, hand lens, computer, reference materials, etc.) to gather and analyze data, with only minor errors.	Used a strategy that led to completion of the investigation/ task. Recorded all data. Used effective scientific reasoning. Framed or used testable questions, conducted experiment, and supported results with data.	A clear explanation was presented. Effectively used scientific representations and notations to organize and display information. Appropriately used data to support conclusions.	Appropriately used scientific terminology. Provided evidence of understanding of relevant scientific concepts, principles or theories (big ideas). Evidence of understanding observable characteristics and properties of objects, organisms, and/or materials used.
Expert	Accurately and proficiently used all appropriate tools and technologies (e.g., rulers, pH paper, hand lens, computer, reference materials, etc.) to gather and analyze data.	Used a sophisticated strategy and revised strategy where appropriate to complete the task. Employed refined and complex reasoning and demonstrated understanding of cause and effect. Applied scientific method accurately: (framed testable questions, designed experiment, gathered and recorded data, analyzed data, and verified results).	Provided clear, effective explanation detailing how the task was carried out. The reader does not need to infer how and why decisions were made. Precisely and appropriately used multiple scientific representations and notations to organize and display information. Interpretation of data supported conclusions, and raised new questions or was applied to new contexts. Disagreements with data resolved when appropriate.	Precisely and appropriately used scientific terminology. Provided evidence of in-depth, sophisticated understanding of relevant scientific concepts, principles or theories (big ideas). Revised prior misconceptions when appropriate. Observable characteristics and properties of objects, organisms, and/or materials used went beyond the task investigation to make other connections or extend thinking.

General Conceptual Understanding Rubric (Grades 5–12)

Conceptual understanding is the extent to which students understand the content to be learned.

High

A high score in conceptual understanding means that the student shows an accurate and extensive understanding of the topic. This can be shown in many ways, including the following:

- Correct and precise use of terminology.
- Precise selection of the pieces of information required to make a point (no more, no less).
- Correct and appropriate use of examples and counterexamples.
- Few errors in information.
- Connections made to other, related topics.
- Demonstration of which distinctions are important to make.
- Key concepts identified and addressed.
- A relevant focus sustained throughout the work.
- Relevant use of a diagram or graph; knows when such things will aid understanding.
- Concise explanations that are to the point.

Medium

A medium score in conceptual understanding means that the student presents some important information, but there is a sense that the student is only about halfway home in terms of understanding. Performance is indicated by the following:

- Reasonably clear ideas, but the reader needs to make some guesses as to what the student meant.
- Even though a general point is made, the student hasn't fine tuned the topic.

- Some parts of the work seem repetitive.
- The balance in the work seems a little off.
- Some vocabulary is used well, some is not.
- Some examples and graphics are appropriate, some aren't.
- Sometimes the student seems to know which concepts and points are most important and telling; other times not.
- Information seems to be based on retelling rather than the student making his or her own connections.
- The focus tends to shift.

Low

A low score in conceptual understanding indicates that the student is still searching for the connections that will make the content meaningful. Weak performance is indicated by such things as the following:

- Ideas are extremely limited or hard to understand, even when the reader tries to draw inferences based on what is there.
- The text may be repetitious or read like a collection of disconnected, random thoughts.
- Information is inaccurate.
- Terminology is used incorrectly.
- There is little sense of which information is most important.
- Visual displays, when used, are not helpful or unrelated to any points the student is trying to make.

Research Paper Rubric (Grades 7–College)

High	Average	Low
Communication	*Communication*	*Communication*
• An inviting introduction draws the reader in, a satisfying conclusion leaves the reader with a sense of closure and resolution;	• The paper has a recognizable introduction and conclusion, but the introduction may not create a strong sense of anticipation and/or the conclusion may not tie the paper into a coherent whole;	• There is no real lead-in to set up what follows, no real conclusion to wrap things up;
• there is a clear thesis;	• there is a thesis but it is ambiguous or unfocused;	• there is no clear thesis; connections between ideas are often confusing or missing;
• transitions are thoughtful and clearly show how ideas connect;	• transitions often work well, but some leave connections between ideas fuzzy;	• citations are infrequent, lack credibility, or often fail to support the author's points;
• uses an appropriate variety of valid sources which are well integrated and support the author's points;	• valid sources generally support the author's points but a greater variety or more detail is needed;	• quotations, paraphrases, and summaries tend to break the flow of the piece, become monotonous, don't seem to fit, and/or are not cited;
• quotations, paraphrases, and summaries are used and cited appropriately;	• quotations, paraphrases, and summaries generally work but occasionally interfere with the flow of the writing, seem irrelevant or are incorrectly cited;	• frequent errors in format or incorrect format used;
• uses the proper format (APA, MLA, etc.);	• uses the proper format but there are occasional errors;	• sequencing seems illogical, disjointed, or forced;
• sequencing is logical and effective; spelling is generally correct, even on more difficult words;	• sequencing shows some logic but it is not under complete control and may be so predictable that the reader finds it distracting;	• there are frequent spelling errors even on common words;
• punctuation is reasonably accurate, consistent, and guides the reader effectively through the text;	• spelling is generally correct but more difficult words may be misspelled;	• punctuation is often missing or incorrect and makes the paper noticeably more difficult to interpret;
• grammar and usage contribute to the clarity; conventions, if manipulated for stylistic effect, work;	• punctuation is acceptable but occasional errors interrupt the flow or confuse the reader;	• errors in grammar or usage are frequent enough to become distracting and interfere with meaning;
• voice and style are appropriate for the type of paper assigned;	• there are problems with grammar or usage but not serious enough to distort meaning;	• voice and style are not appropriate for the type of paper assigned;
• paragraphs are well-focused and coherent.	• voice and style don't quite fit with the type of paper assigned; paragraphs occasionally lack focus or coherence.	• paragraphs generally lack focus or coherence.

High	Average	Low
Critical Thinking	*Critical Thinking*	*Critical Thinking*
• The paper displays insight and originality of thought;	• There are some original ideas and some seem obvious or elementary;	• There are few original ideas, most seem obvious or elementary;
• there is sound and logical analysis that reveals clear understanding of the relevant issues;	• analysis is generally sound but there are lapses in logic or understanding;	• analysis is superficial or illogical; the author seems to struggle to understand the relevant issues;
• there is an appropriate balance of factual reporting, interpretation and analysis, and personal opinion;	• the balance among factual reporting, interpretation and analysis, and personal opinion seems skewed;	• there is a clear imbalance among factual reporting, interpretation and analysis, and personal opinion;
• the author goes beyond the obvious in constructing interpretation of the facts;	• paper shows understanding of relevant issues but lacks depth;	• author appears to misunderstand or omit key issues;
• telling and accurate details are used to reinforce the author's arguments;	• generally accurate details are included but the reader is left with questions—more information is needed to "fill in the blanks";	• there are few details or most details seem irrelevant;
• the paper is convincing and satisfying.	• the paper leaves the reader vaguely skeptical and unsatisfied.	• the paper leaves the reader unconvinced.

High	Average	Low
Content	*Content*	*Content*
• The paper addresses a topic within the context of examining biological, personal, social/cultural/political, or paradigmatic change;	• The paper addresses a topic within the appropriate context but the connections are somewhat tenuous or there are diversions to less relevant points;	• The paper addresses a topic only vaguely related to examining change;
• the paper is complete and leaves no important aspect of the topic not addressed;	• the paper is substantially complete but one or more important aspects of the topic are not addressed;	• the paper is clearly incomplete with many important aspects of the topic left out;
• the author has a good grasp of what is known, what is generally accepted, and what is yet to be discovered;	• the author has a good grasp of the relevant information, but fails to distinguish among what is known, what is generally accepted, and what is yet to be discovered;	• the author has a poor grasp of the relevant information;
• appropriate significance is assigned to the information presented and irrelevant information is rarely included;	• the paper often uses information in a way inappropriate to its significance or includes much irrelevant information;	• the paper frequently uses information inappropriately or uses irrelevant information;
• connections between the topic of the paper and related topics are made that enhance understanding;	• there are few connections made to related topics;	• no connections are made to related topics to help clarify the information presented;
• specialized terminology, if used, is used correctly and precisely;	• specialized terminology is sometimes incorrectly or imprecisely used;	• specialized terminology is frequently misused;
• the author seems to be writing from personal and/or professional knowledge or experience.	• the author seems to be writing from knowledge or experience but has difficulty going from general observations to specifics.	• the work seems to be a simple restatement of the assignment or a simple, overly broad answer to a question with little evidence of expertise on the part of the author.

Seminar Discussion Rubric (Grades 5–12)

4 *Perceptive*

Contributes insightful comments. Makes connections between experiences or events within the text and to experiences or events in other texts and/or situations. Uses sufficient evidence from the text to support interpretations and assertions. Asks open-ended questions that stimulate discussion. Challenges to others' ideas are elaborated with reasoned evidence. Speaks directly to other students during discussion. Comments reflect examination of other students' contributions. Builds on thoughts of others. Responds to challenges and questions with further information, or refines own interpretations to accommodate new perceptions or information. Maintains engagement throughout the discussion. The student's word usage, grammar, and sentence structure are correct and are chosen to enhance meaning.

3 *Thoughtful/Functional*

The student maintains engagement throughout the discussion. Contributions reflect consideration of the ideas in the text and of ideas expressed by others during the discussion. Speaks directly to other students during discussion. Supports interpretations with evidence from the text. May occasionally make connections between experiences or events within the text and to experiences or events in other texts and/or situations. Responds to challenges and questions with further information, or refines own interpretations to accommodate new perceptions or information. Questions others' interpretations.

2 *Sporadic*

Some comments focus on the topic of discussion, but some include unrelated ideas with no attempt to connect them to the discussion or to the text. Support for assertions may be attempted, but may not go far enough, may be unrelated to the assertion, or may be inaccurate. The student may direct comments or questions to the teacher rather than to other students. When challenged, the student may not be able to offer support for interpretations; or, responds to questions by reasserting the idea being questioned. Comments may ignore other students' contributions. Comments may interrupt the student speaking. The student may have difficulty using vocabulary correctly or may have difficulty with sentence structure: the way words and phrases are strung together may be incorrect or convoluted so that meaning is obscured at times. The student may also make some grammatical errors.

1 Dysfunctional/Uninvolved

The student does not contribute to the discussion. Or, if offered, contributions disrupt rather than further discussion through one or more of the following problems.

- They appear significantly unrelated to the flow of ideas in the discussion or to the text and the student makes no attempt to explain their relevance.

- They express criticism focused on attributes of other students rather than on attributes of their ideas.

- They represent a significant misunderstanding of the text.

- They make assertions with no attempt at credible support. Or if support is attempted, it reveals a lack of understanding of what constitutes credible support.

- They interrupt a student while speaking.

- They are hard to understand because of incorrect word meanings, grammar, and/or sentence structure.

Technical Writing Rubric (Grades 5–12)

Trait 1: Content, Focus, and Purpose

5 *The purpose of the writing is immediately clear. The writing is focused and informative.*

The information is concise, not overwhelming, and focuses on a key issue or a few related issues.

The information is clear, complete, and accurate.

The facts or claims are thoroughly substantiated.

The content and amount of information are well suited to the intended audience.

The reader's questions are anticipated and addressed.

3 *The purpose of the writing can be inferred through careful reading. The writing provides some useful information and is focused primarily on one target topic or issue.*

The information is clear, though not necessarily complete or always accurate.

Not all facts or claims are substantiated.

The information is not always suited to the intended audience.

Irrelevant information is included, or there is not enough substance.

Some of the reader's questions are anticipated and addressed.

1 *The purpose of the writing is difficult to infer, or the writing itself is loosely focused and is not targeted to any clear issue or topic.*

The information is unclear, incomplete, or inaccurate.

The facts or claims are generally unsubstantiated.

The information does not seem suited to the intended audience, or it is difficult to tell who the audience might be.

The information is too skimpy, too scattered, or unfocused.

The reader's questions are not anticipated or addressed.

Trait 2: Organizational Structure

5 *Information is presented in a way that is both engaging and informative.*

The first words capture the reader's attention and hint at the content to come.

The main points stand out.

Key information is easy to spot.

The order of the information makes interpretation of the whole message easy.

Purposeful transitions connect each part of the main idea and connect the points to one another.

The writing concludes with information the reader needs to know and remember, or it provides for a call to action.

3 *Information is presented in a reasonably straightforward manner.*

The text makes an early connection to the main message.

The main points can be inferred, but do not stand out.

Key information can be located with a little work.

The order of information is occasionally confusing or puzzling, but still supports the reader's understanding of the overall picture.

Transitions are evident; however, not all points are connected to the main idea or to each other.

The conclusion provides only a limited sense of closure or resolution.

I *Lack of organization leaves the reader confused about what is most important.*

It is difficult to connect the introduction to any overall purpose.

The main points are buried, not highlighted, and may be hard to infer.

The key information is difficult to locate.

The presentation seems random and does not support the reader's understanding.

Transitions are lacking or inappropriate; ideas do not connect to the main idea or to one another.

The writing lacks a sense of closure or resolution; at the end, nothing stands out as most important in the reader's mind.

Trait 3: Style and Terminology

5 *The style and tone reflect the writer's engagement with the topic and a concern for the audience. The language is fully appropriate to both topic and audience.*

The writer seems committed to his or her topic.

The writer's voice holds the reader's attention—but also is appropriate for the topic, audience, and purpose.

The language is clear and unambiguous; it contributes to the reader's understanding.

Sentences are worded in a straightforward manner that helps make the main point clear and obvious.

The text includes sentences, or phrases where appropriate, that are somewhat varied in length and structure.

Technical terms and specialized vocabulary are used only when necessary and appropriate and are explained as needed.

3 *The style and tone reflect the writer's comfort with the topic, but do not suggest enthusiasm. The language at times is inflated with jargon or is too simple for the audience, the topic, or both.*

The writer seems somewhat interested in his or her topic.

The writer's voice attempts to hold the reader's attention, or it may be inappropriate (e.g., too formal, too chatty) for the topic, audience, and/or purpose.

The language occasionally is unclear or ambiguous; the reader sometimes needs more clarification, the definition of a term, or just a good, clear example.

Most sentences are worded in a straightforward manner that helps make the main point clear and obvious.

The text often includes sentences, or phrases where appropriate, that are somewhat varied in length and structure.

Technical terms are sometimes used when they are not needed, or the language lacks the precision needed for the content area.

1 *The style and tone reflect the writer's discomfort with and/or apparent indifference to the topic. The language tends to be too general to give the reader the information s/he needs; or it is so inflated with jargon that it is almost impossible to understand.*

The writer seems confused by, or uninterested in, his or her topic.

The writer does not seem to speak to any particular audience, or the tone and language seem unsuited to the audience and/or purpose.

The language is unclear, ambiguous, or too general; the reader may feel buried in jargon or that nothing has been clarified or explained.

Sentences are convoluted.

Sentences and phrases are not varied in length and structure.

Technical terminology clutters the text, or the language is too general for the complexity of the topic.

Trait 4: Format, Layout, and Conventions

5 *The writer creates a visually effective layout. Graphics and typographic devices, if used, make the text as visually appealing as the context requires. Editing is thorough.*

The layout is attractive, effective, and appropriate. It is balanced and clearly laid out, with good use of easy-on-the-eyes white space.

Key ideas stand out because of the writer's effective use of typographic devices, when needed, including

- Boldface
- Italics, underlining, and bullets
- Variations in font, style, and size

Key ideas are stated in sentences, clauses, or phrases, and are parallel in form.

Outside sources are cited correctly according to the format for the content area.

The writer uses graphics (illustrations, charts, graphs, etc.), when needed, to help the reader interpret data or draw conclusions.

The text is carefully edited and is free of errors in spelling, punctuation, grammar, paragraphing, and capitalization.

3 *The writer creates a visually coordinated presentation with enough attention to layout, graphics, and typographic devices, when needed, to make the text readable.*

The layout is appropriate and tends to highlight key ideas. It is appropriate to both purpose and audience.

The writer occasionally, but somewhat randomly, makes use of typographic devices, when needed, including
- Boldface
- Italics, underlining, and bullets
- Variations in font, style, and size

Key ideas are generally stated in sentences, clauses, or phrases, and some are parallel in form.

Outside sources are cited.

The use of graphics is minimal or not as clear as the reader would like.

The text, though edited, still contains some noticeable errors in spelling, punctuation, grammar, paragraphing, and capitalization.

1 *Attention to layout, graphics, and typographic devices is minimal. Editing clearly needs work.*

The layout is cluttered or visually confusing, or the paper simply has a rough-draft look.

The writer rarely, if ever, makes use of typographic devices, even when they would create emphasis or help key points stand out.

Key ideas are not presented in any consistent format.

Outside sources are not cited.

Graphics are needed, but are not used, or they create more confusion than understanding.

The text contains many noticeable and distracting errors in spelling, punctuation, grammar, paragraphing, and capitalization.

Teaming Rubric (Grades 7–College)

This is a composite rubric synthesized from several sources. It is not meant to be a checklist—the descriptors under each level of performance are indicators of the quality of the performance rather than an exhaustive listing; not everything must be "checked off" to receive a score of a particular level. The rubric should be considered a work in progress. The work by Larson and LeFasto (*Teamwork: What Must Go Right/What Can Go Wrong*, London, UK: Sage, 1989) is the principal source for elements of quality identified in the rubric.

Trait 1: Collaborative Climate

Guiding questions:

- Does the team create a working environment that promotes trust, open communication, and synergy?
- Does the team recognize and use the strengths of each individual?

Level 5 The team establishes and maintains the environment needed for equal participation from all team members.

- Leadership within the team is based on intrinsic human values such as trust, cheerfulness, loyalty, friendliness, courtesy, kindness, thrift, and respect ("principled leadership").
- The team uses processes that reveal the strengths of each individual and they create a shared understanding of how each individual contributes.
- The team uses forward-focused evaluation.
- The team uses processes that ensure that each voice is heard and valued.
- Conflicts between team members are brought to the team for resolution. The team employs a conflict resolution process that solves the problems and promotes collaboration.

- The team requires effective listening practices of its members. This includes traits such as acknowledging, attending, reflecting, probing, summarizing, etc.

Level 3 The team is aware of the need for an appropriate environment, but lacks the skills to establish it.

- The team works to have meaningful, specific reviews of performance that promote genuine improvement, but sometimes fail in their efforts.

- Some team members can identify individual member's strengths, but the team doesn't benefit from it because the strengths are not utilized.

- The team aims for forward-focused evaluations, but periodically falls short.

- New ideas are encouraged and sometimes considered fairly, or, at times, idea synthesis fails because all ideas are viewed as equally credible even after their consideration.

- Occasionally, some voices are not heard. Sometimes the dominant member rules the discussion or the quiet, shy member remains that way, or the concerns go unmentioned to provide "harmony" in the team.

- Conflicts are identified, but not effectively dealt with because of lacking skills or processes. The team values conflict for team development but lacks ability in harnessing its potential.

- Listening for understanding practices occur (roughly 50% of the time).

Level 1 The team does not consider an environment where each opinion is given equal consideration valuable.

- The team does not review their performance, or they do it only when required to do so.

- All team members are unaware of the strengths of their teammates, or they believe that their idea is always the best method.

- Evaluations are negative; they focus on what is wrong, and fail to make suggestions for improvement.
- When a new idea emerges, it is routinely shot down.
- Frequently, some voices are not heard. One or several team members may dominate the conversation, a reflective or shy team member may fail to state their viewpoint, or in the interests of "harmony" a team member may not voice a concern.
- Conflicts are ignored or denied. The team believes that their focus should be "to all get along."
- Listening for understanding rarely occurs.

Trait 2: Performance Development

Guiding questions:

- Does the team strive for excellence?
- Does the team hold individuals accountable for their performance?
- Is there a focus on growth in performance for both the team and the individual?

Level 5 The team is constantly striving to improve overall team performance.

- The team has a process for continuous improvement. This means they regularly and routinely evaluate many aspects of individual and team performance. In addition they implement ideas for improvement, and demonstrate improved performance over time.
- The team uses roles to continuously develop the individuals' talents and enhance team performance.
- The team holds individuals accountable for their performance.

- The team strives to become an asset to the organization, supervisor, or other relevant entity.
- The team embraces and takes on increasingly challenging tasks.

Level 3 The team considers their performance when encouraged by an outside source.

- The team considers their continuous improvement important but lacks adequate skills to effect change. They evaluate some aspects of individual and team performance. They implement some ideas for improvement, and show fairly small performance improvement over time.
- The team can relate to the use of roles in developing individuals' talents and enhancing team performance, but lacks skills in establishing or using roles.
- The team has a method of accountability for individual member performance, but it is semi-effective.
- The team sees how they could benefit the organization, supervisor, or other relevant entity.
- The team accepts increasingly challenging tasks as part of their duty as a team.

Level 1 The team never formally considers their performance.

- The team does not consider their continuous improvement. They do not evaluate any aspects of individual and team performance. They do not implement ideas for improvement because none are generated, and do not show performance improvement over time.
- The team is unconcerned with developing individuals' talents and enhancing team performance.
- The team has no method of accountability for individual member performance.

- The team does not see how they could benefit the organization, supervisor, or other relevant entity.
- The team shuns increasingly challenging tasks.

Trait 3: Infrastructure

Guiding questions:

- Has the team established ways to work together and to use resources?
- Does the team create goals that appeal and connect with each individual?

Level 5 The team has chosen methods to govern their work and help each member improve.

- The team creates goals that appeal to each individual and that help create an atmosphere where team goals are more important than individual goals (unified commitment).
- The team has well understood expectations (e.g., defined levels of quality, on time to meetings, acceptable contribution, etc.).
- The team continually adapts plans and processes to meet the changing needs of the stakeholders involved.
- The team matches the environment and resources to the task (i.e., shop for manufacturing, conference room for client meetings, etc.).
- The team follows effective meeting practices. This means meetings have clear objectives, have an agenda, are documented appropriately, begin/end on time, stay on task, and meeting time management is appropriate.
- The team has a process for deciding if tasks are best done as a team or individually.

Level 3 The team has some methods to govern their work and help members improve.

- The team has goals that are accepted by many team members, but not all members are committed to their realization.

- The team has developed expectations that appeal to most teammates.

- The team tries to adapt plans and processes to meet the changing needs of the stakeholders involved, but sometimes fails because of poor skills or lack of consensus.

- The team considers the impact of environment and resources on successful task completion. They are developing the ability to match tasks with the environment and resources appropriately.

- The team is developing their meeting practice. The meetings have about 50% of the elements important to good meetings (i.e. objectives, agendas, appropriate documentation, etc). They are developing abilities in managing time during the meetings.

- The team is developing skills in determining whether work is best done as a team or individually.

Level 1 The team has no methods to govern their work or help each member improve.

- The team has no goals. There is no sense of unity or commitment.

- The team has not discussed expectations of the team members.

- The team will not adapt plans and processes to meet the changing needs of the stakeholders involved.

- The team never considers the impact of environment and resources on successful task completion.

- The team has no meeting practice. Meetings lack objectives, agendas, and appropriate documentation. They do not begin/ end on time or stay on task. During meetings, time management is non-evident.

- The team has not yet developed skills in deciding whether work is best done as a team or individually.

Trait 4: Project Focus

Guiding questions:

- Does the team have clear and elevating goals?
- Is the team focused on creating results?
- Does the team consider the broad societal impacts of their work?

Level 5 The team has clear, compelling goals that elevate each member to a new level of performance.

- Team goals are elevating and clearly understood by each member and by relevant stakeholders. In addition team goals satisfy other criteria such those described by the SMART* acronym.

- The team considers engineering ethics. This includes loyalty to employers, societal issues and impacts, design for the environment, health, safety, and similar issues.

- The team is results-oriented. They routinely and continuously create appropriate results in the process of completing a project.

- The superior quality of the team's work generates external support and recognition.

---

*Attributed to Rick DuFour (ATI conference, 2002), SMART is an acronym for Strategic and specific, Measurable, Attainable, Results-oriented, and Time-bound.

Level 3 The team is developing skills in creating clear, compelling goals that will elevate the performance of all members.

- Team goals are clearly understood by each member and by relevant stakeholders, but are not yet elevating (or vice versa). Team goals satisfy many of the other criteria such those described by the SMART acronym (the goals are SAT, SMT, or ART, etc).

- The team considers some elements of engineering ethics. This includes loyalty to employers, societal issues and impacts, design for the environment, health, safety, and similar issues.

- The team is becoming results-oriented. They sometimes create appropriate results in the process of completing a project.

- The team's work generates internal support and recognition.

Level 1 The team has no goals, or the goals do not elevate team members' performance.

- Team goals are either not established or do not agree with the view of relevant stakeholders.

- Team goals do not satisfy other criteria such as those described by the SMART acronym.

- The team never considers engineering ethics. There is no conversation about loyalty to employers, societal issues and impacts, design for the environment, health, safety and similar issues.

- The team has not developed a results-oriented view of design. They routinely and continuously create inappropriate or inadequate results in the process of completing a project.

- The poor quality of the team's work prevents future external support and recognition of the team.

Trait 5: Personal Responsibility

Guiding question:

- Does everyone personally strive to maintain the high performance of the team?

Level 5 The individual demonstrates responsible and professional behavior.

- The team member is on time to team activities (as described by the team standards).

- The team member gives positive and forward-focused comments.

- The team member completes tasks on schedule and with a level of performance that is judged high quality by the team.

- The team member appropriately voices their viewpoint on all team issues.

- The team member assumes leadership and responsibility on subtasks.

- The team member accepts a role and is open to rotation of roles to promote individual growth.

- Instead of spinning their wheels, the team member brings both technical and people problems to the team.

- The team member places highest priority on team success rather than on personal benefits or acclaim.

- The team member makes an adequate and appropriate contribution to the team.

Level 3 The individual demonstrates some responsible and professional behavior.

- The team member is sometimes late or misses team activities.

- The team member occasionally spouts "killer-phrases." Positive comments occur about ½ of the time.

- The team member points out problems with other's viewpoint and gives some ideas for improvement.
- The team member completes some assigned tasks, or the quality of their completed work is not always acceptable to the team and must be reworked.
- The team member sometimes dominates the discussion or sometimes fails to voice their point of view.
- The team member assumes dutiful responsibility on many tasks.
- The team member is willing to accept roles, yet struggles to understand why they are rotated.
- The team member tries not to spin their wheels, but still gets "locked in" on some problems.
- The team member is somewhat concerned with the team's success.
- The team member makes a half-hearted contribution to the team.

Level 1 The individual demonstrates irresponsible and non-professional behavior.

- The team member is often late or misses team activities.
- The team member regularly spouts "killer-phrases." These are comments that are negative, cynical, derogatory, or overly critical.
- The team member points out problems with the viewpoints or ideas of others without giving forward-focused recommendations.
- The team member fails to complete assigned tasks, or the quality of their completed work is not acceptable to the team and must be reworked.
- The team member dominates the discussion or the team member fails to voice their point of view.

- The team member does not assume responsibility on any tasks.
- The team member is unwilling to accept roles.
- The team member spends far too much time trying to solve problems alone instead of asking for help when they get stuck.
- The team member is most concerned with their personal agenda and success.
- The team member makes little contribution to the team.

Reading Developmental Continuum (Primary)
Learning to Read, Learning to Listen

	Level A: Pre-emergent	Level B: Emergent	Level C: Beginning
Comprehension	• Uses pictorial cues when sharing a book or "reading," e.g., points to a picture in *The Three Little Pigs* says, "The three little pigs left home." • Talks about favorite stories. • Demonstrates understanding of television programs, oral stories or picture books by connecting them to own knowledge and experiences.	• May tell a story from pictures. • Predicts meaning of environmental symbols or messages (e.g., recurrent "Stop" signs, McDonald's symbol, etc). • Tells/draws personal stories in sequence. • Listens to and retells stories in sequence.	• Recognizes when the reading isn't making sense. • Recounts sequence of events. • Listens to stories and responds. *Mark continuum based on secure, habituated, independent behavior of student*

Skills/Strategies	• Recognizes own name in a variety of print.
	• Displays reading-like behavior:
	  – holds the book the right way up
	  – turns the pages appropriately
	  – looks at words and pictures
	  – uses pictures to construct ideas
	• Understands that print is read from top to bottom of page and left page before right page.
	• Responds to and uses simple terminology such as: book, right way up, front, back, upside down.
		• Recognizes most letter sounds.
		• Recognizes parts of own name in print (e.g., Sam says, "That's my name" pointing to 'Stop' sign).
		• Knows several words by sight (mom, I, stop, dad, friends' names).
		• Relies primarily on memory for reading.
		• May invent text with book language.
		• Focuses on pictures for meaning rather than print.
		• Knows that both pictures and text exist.
		• Understands that print is read from left to right on a page.
			• Uses initial and/or final letter and sounds to predict a word.
			• Locates/reads known words (sight words).
			• Begins to use context, grammatical, and/or phonics cues.
			• Matches words spoken to words in print (1-1 match).
			• Stops at an unknown word.
			• Looks at print and pictures.
			• Understands the difference between a sentence, word, letter.
			• Understands that print carries meaning.
			• Knows concepts of beginning, middle, and end.
			• Begins to read in phrases as opposed to word by word.

Learning to Read, Learning to Listen

	Level A: Pre-emergent	Level B: Emergent	Level C: Beginning
Attitudes/Behaviors	• Displays curiosity about print by experimenting with scribble writing and drawing and asking, "What does that say?" • Looks at books. • Chooses and enjoys hearing a variety of favorite books. • Eagerly responds to book-reading events (plays, flannel board, puppets).	• Asks questions or comments about print in the environment. • Actively participates in the oral/shared reading of familiar stories (e.g., joins in on familiar refrains, patterns, or phrases in books or poems). • Wants to read text and points to text in general. • May pretend to read.	• Is willing to read. • Focuses on print, supported by pictures. • Vocalizes when reading. • Uses appropriate listening behaviors.

← – – – – – – – – – – Kindergarten Range: A to C – – – – – →

← ——————————————— First Grade Range: B–F ———→

239

Learning to Read, Learning to Listen

	Level D: Early Developing	Level E: Developing	Level F
Comprehension	• Predicts what will happen next. • Recalls main ideas and details. • Orally connects own experiences to reading.	• Retells story in sequence. • Summarizes story. • Backs up literal statements with proof from story. • Forms an opinion about a story.	• Orally responds to questions about character; setting, problem, and solution. • Understands the use of exaggeration. • Distinguishes fact from fiction. • Demonstrates knowledge of the function of chapters.
Skills/Strategies	• Uses word parts to read unknown words (e.g., endings—s, ed, ing; blends—sp, bl, st; digraphs—ch, sh, th; and simple word families—...at,...ad,...op). • Increases sight word vocabulary. • Increases and refines use of context, grammatical, and/or phonics cues. • Begins to use a variety of ways of cross checking. • Begins to self-correct errors. • Pauses at appropriate places when reading orally. • Uses a period, question mark, and exclamation mark when reading.	• Begins to solve unknown words by using word families (...ate,...eat,...een, etc). • Uses beginning, middle, and final letter sounds to read unknown word. • Increases sight word vocabulary. • Cross checking is automatic. • When rereading, confidently reads a story with appropriate expression. • Uses quotation marks and commas when reading.	• Solves unknown words by using syllables or meaningful word parts (e.g., root words—tie, do, read; prefixes—un, re, pre; and suffixes— ful, ly, est). • Increases sight word vocabulary. • Self-corrects automatically. • Reads orally with expression or with appropriate pauses.
Attitudes/Behaviors	• Independently selects books to look at/read. • Reads familiar books. • Participates in oral/shared reading of both fiction and nonfiction.	• Reads for pleasure or information. • Shows familiarity with titles and authors. • May read silently, sometimes vocalizing when text is difficult. • Actively responds to books.	• May recommend books to others. • Chooses and locates library books. • Reads silently.

‹ – – – First Grade Range: B–F – – – ›

‹——— Second Grade Range: D to H ———›

Learning to Read, Learning to Listen / Reading to Learn, Listening to Learn

	Level G	Level H: Benchmark 3	Level I
Comprehension	• Orally responds to literature questions and is beginning to respond in writing. • Identifies and interprets characters' interactions. • Recognizes and retains specialized vocabulary (e.g., unusual names, unfamiliar terms/concepts). • Understands idiomatic expressions (...fur looked like mashed prunes). • Retains story line through episodes or longer chapter books.	• Summarizes major events. • Identifies character, setting, and plot. • Evaluates characters, authors, and books. • Uses information to draw conclusions. • Recalls word meaning by giving an example. • Notices author's choices of words. • Compares ideas read to prior knowledge. • Listens and responds orally to other's opinions and questions about a text. • Knows how to question self before, during, and after reading.	• Connects ideas to make inferences, draw conclusions, and predict what will happen next. • Recalls word meanings by giving a definition. • Recognizes effective use of word choice by an author for a specific purpose. • Listens and responds to fiction and nonfiction in writing, discussions, storytelling/performance, and so forth. • Interprets fiction read by retelling and discussing plot, characters, setting, and events. • Interprets nonfiction, citing main ideas and supporting details. • Paraphrases/retells passages. • Supports opinions about text with evidence from text and own life.

Skills/Strategies	• Uses word identification strategies appropriately and automatically when encountering an unknown word.
	• Retains high frequency words as part of sight word vocabulary.
		• Integrates reading strategies fluently and effectively.
		• Reads contractions and abbreviations.
		• Identifies and uses:
		  – title page
		  – table of contents
		  – index
		  – author, illustrator
		• Adjusts reading rate to meet the demands of the text.
			• Rereads, scans, and skims text for specific information.
			• Analyzes parts of words and sentence context to problem solve new words.
			• Uses references for specific research purposes.
			• Uses text organizations such as chapters, paragraphs, and conclusions.
			• Identifies and uses:
			  – glossary
			  – copyright

(Mark continuum based on secure, habituated, independent behavior of student)

Learning to Read, Learning to Listen / Reading to Learn, Listening to Learn

	Level G	Level H: Benchmark 3	Level I
Attitudes/Behaviors	• Chooses to read a variety of materials for a variety of purposes. • Uses active listening skills during oral reading of fiction and nonfiction.	• Knows own reading preferences. • Selects texts at his/her reading level.	• Reflects and evaluates self as a reader. • Self-motivated to read for pleasure.

← – – – – Second Grade Range: D to H – – – – – →

← – – – – Third Grade Range: G to I – – – – – →

← ———— Fourth Grade Range: H to K ———— →

← ———— Fifth Grade Range: I to K ———— →

Reading to Learn, Listening to Learn

Level J	Level K: Benchmark 5
• Makes inferences based on ideas in text and provides justification for the inferences. • Begins to use content vocabulary in speaking and writing. • Recognizes that authors use specific words to convey a feeling, tone, and emotional state. • Connects ideas from reading to universal themes such as friendship, tolerance, and community.	• Comprehends texts that may be removed from personal experience. • Begins to use content vocabulary in reference to real life situations. • Interprets author's use of specific words/phrases that convey feeling, tone, and emotional states. • Identifies figurative language such as simile, metaphor, onomatopoeia, and alliteration. • Recognizes devices in a text that indicate stereotyped characters and suggests ways in which stereotypical characters might be changed. • Compares universal themes between texts read. • Infers, predicts, and generalizes, citing evidence from the text. • Confirms, extends, or amends own knowledge through reading.
• Selects and uses a variety of reference materials for specific research purposes. • Uses a variety of text structures (letter, narrative, report, recount) and text organizations (bold print, key word, caption).	• Selects appropriate material and adjusts reading strategies for different texts and purposes (skimming to search for a fact, scanning for a key word, headings). • Reads and uses content specific vocabulary (e.g., in science, math, technology).
• Generates personal questions and discussion about self as a reader. • May discover a particular genre and may seek out other titles of this type.	• Analyzes self as a reader. • Sees books as useful sources of information.

←- - - - - - - - - - - - - - - - - - - Fourth Grade Range: H to K - - - - →

←——————— Fifth Grade Range: I to K ————————→

243

Oral Presentation Rubric (Grades 4–12)

Criterion 1: Content

Strong	Middle	Weak
Ideas are focused and supported with relevant details and examples. Content is relevant for the task.	The topic is fairly broad, but is focused on relevant content. Support is attempted, but doesn't go far enough.	There is little controlling idea, the speaker is still in search of a topic, or the length is not adequate for development.
Information is accurate.	Ideas are reasonably clear, but there are some problems with accuracy.	Information is limited, unclear, or incorrect.
The speaker has chosen the most significant information and stays with the topic.	The speaker generally stays on the topic, but doesn't develop a clear theme.	Everything seems as important as everything else.
The speaker anticipates the information needs of the audience, adapts content to the listeners' background, and/or refers to listeners' experience.	The listener is left with questions. There seems to be some "holes" in the information.	The presentation may be repetitious or sound like a collection of disconnected thoughts.

Criterion 2: Organization

Strong	Middle	Weak
The speaker helps the listener understand the sequence of ideas through organizational aids such as previewing the organization, using transitions, and summarizing. Listeners can put the ideas in an outline.	The sequence and relationships are fairly easy to follow, but sometimes you have to make assumptions to connect the ideas. An outline of the ideas requires inferences.	Ideas that go together are not put together. Listeners would have trouble putting the ideas into an outline.
The opening draws the listener in; the closing leaves a sense of closure and resolution.	The presentation has a recognizable opening and closing, but there is little sense of anticipation or closure.	There is no opening or closing.
Details seem to fit where they're placed.	Sequencing is sometimes awkward. Some details don't seem to fit where they're placed.	Sequencing is confusing.

Criterion 3: Delivery

Strong	Middle	Weak
Volume is loud enough to be heard and understood. Volume is intentionally used to keep the listener's attention and/or enhance the points being made.	The speaker can be heard and volume doesn't distract the listener, but neither does volume draw attention to important points.	The speaker can't be heard and/or changes in volume distract the listener from understanding the points being made.
Visual aids are used effectively to support and enhance meaning.	Visual aids, while understandable, don't add much to the presentation.	Visual aids are confusing, do not relate to the point being made, or distract the listener.
Pronunciation and enunciation are clear enough to be understood and are used to emphasize important points.	Pronunciation and/or enunciation are generally clear enough to be understood, but are not used effectively to underscore important points.	Pronunciation and/or enunciation detract from being able to understand the speaker.
The speaker exhibits very few disfluencies, such as "ah," "um," and "you know."	While the speaker exhibits disfluencies, they don't detract from the presentation enough to interfere with meaning.	Disfluencies, such as "um," "ah," and "you know," detract from understanding what is being said.
There is little in the presenter's demeanor, dress, or mannerisms that distract the listener from the message	The presenter's demeanor, dress, or mannerisms sometimes distract the listener, but meaning is not disrupted.	The presenter's demeanor, dress, or mannerisms distract the listener to the extent that meaning is disrupted.
Pacing is right for the audience. The speaker knows when to slow down and when to speed up.	Pacing is fairly good, but at times the speaker goes too fast or too slow for the listeners to keep up.	Pacing is awkward. The listener wants the speaker to either get on it or not go so quickly.
Sentences are varied and easy to listen to and understand. They attract and hold attention.	Sentences are usually correct and can be understood, but generally lack the flair that maintains attention.	Sentences are either ramble, are choppy, or are awkward. Sentence structure might all be the same and so become boring.

Criterion 4: Language Use

Strong	Middle	Weak
Words and phrases are accurate, to the point, create pictures in the listener's head, and/or result in emphasizing the intended points.	The speaker uses bland language that, while not detracting from the message, does little to enhance it.	Grammar and vocabulary detract from being able to understand the speaker's message.
The speaker consciously uses language techniques such as vivid language, emotional language, humor imagery, metaphor, and simile.	Words and grammar are accurate and communicate, but don't capture the listener's attention.	Word and phrases either sound like a thesaurus on the loose or are so nondescript, such as "thing" and "stuff" that the listener looses attention. The speaker might use jargon or clichés. Words are used incorrectly.

Source: Some wording based on the *6 + 1 Trait™ Writing Assessment Scoring Guide;* the oral presentation rubric *On-Demand Speaking* (Massachusetts Department of Education, 1998); and other oral presentation rubrics of unknown provenance. Adapted by permission where applicable.

appendix

Rubric for Tasks

Overview

The *Rubric for Tasks* is a rubric for evaluating the quality of performance tasks. It describes features of a task necessary to obtain the performance or product you intend to assess.

The *Rubric for Tasks* addresses three aspects of quality and is therefore organized into three categories, or criteria, each with its own set of descriptors.

- Criterion 1: *Content of the Task*—What information does the task need to supply to students?

- Criterion 2: *Sampling*—Is there enough evidence to support the intended purpose?

- Criterion 3: *Distortion Due to Bias*—What can interfere with an accurate picture of student achievement?

Each criterion contains one or more descriptors at each of three levels—Strong, Medium, and Weak.

How to Use the *Rubric for Tasks*

This rubric is intended to be used to determine a task's relative strengths and weaknesses for each descriptor. Unlike the *Rubric for Rubrics*, you do not make an overall judgment for each of the criteria (*Content, Sampling,* and *Distortion*). Rather, you determine which level (Strong, Medium, or Weak) of each descriptor matches what you see in the task. The rubric is intended to function diagnostically, to give you an immediate picture of what you would need to revise to make the task strong. We do suggest one summative decision: If the task is not related to the learning targets you intend to assess (the first descriptor under *Content of the Task*), do not continue rating it because you will not want to use it.

Rubric for Tasks

	CRITERION 1: CONTENT OF THE TASK	
	What Information Do Students Need?	
Strong	*Medium*	*Weak*
1. All requirements of the task are directly related to the learning target(s) to be assessed. The task will elicit a performance that could be used to judge proficiency on the intended learning targets.	1. Some requirements of the task are not related to the learning target(s) to be assessed. There is extra work in this task not needed to assess the intended learning targets.	1. Requirements of the task are not related to the learning target(s) to be assessed. The task will not elicit a performance that could be used to judge proficiency on the intended learning targets.
2. The task specifies the following: • The knowledge students are to use in creating the task • The performance or product students are to create—what form it should take • The materials to be used, if any • Timeline for completion	2. Some of the following information is clear; some is unclear or missing: • The knowledge students are to use in creating the task • The performance or product students are to create—what form it should take • The materials to be used, if any • Timeline for completion	2. The task does not specify the following: • The knowledge students are to use in creating the task • The performance or product students are to create—what form it should take • The materials to be used, if any • Timeline for completion
3. Tasks assessing a performance skill specify the conditions under which the performance or demonstration is to take place.	3. Tasks assessing a performance skill do not sufficiently specify the conditions under which the performance or demonstration is to take place.	3. Tasks assessing a performance skill do not at all specify the conditions under which the performance or demonstration is to take place.
4. Multi-day tasks specify the help allowed.	4. Although there is some reference to what kind of help is allowed for multi-day tasks, it could be misinterpreted.	4. Multi-day tasks do not specify the help allowed.
5. The task includes a description of the criteria by which the performance or product will be judged.	5. Although present, the description of the criteria by which the performance or product will be judged is vague or unclear (see *Rubric for Rubrics*).	5. The task includes no reference to the criteria by which the performance or product will be judged.

Rubric for Tasks (Continued)

CRITERION 1: CONTENT OF THE TASK
What Information Do Students Need? (Continued)

Strong	Medium	Weak
6. The content of the task is sufficient to let students know what they are to do without giving so much information that the task will no longer measure level of mastery of the intended learning target. The content points the way to success without doing the thinking for the student.	6. Some parts of the task may give students too much help, compromising the results when they are intended to be used to measure the student's achievement of the learning target independently. In some places, the task does the thinking or the work for the student.	6. The task is over-scaffolded. If used for summative purposes, the task cannot measure students' ability to create the product or performance independently, because the content is so explicit that students can follow it like a recipe. Students can achieve a high score and/or satisfactorily complete the task without having mastered the intended learning target. The task measures only students' ability to follow directions.

CRITERION 2: SAMPLING
Is There Enough Evidence?

Strong	Medium	Weak
1. The number of tasks or repeated instances of performance is sufficient to measure the intended learning target and to support the kind of judgment intended to be made.	1. There are more tasks or repeated instances of performance than are needed to measure the intended learning target or to support the kind of judgment intended to be made.	1. The number of tasks or repeated instances of performance is not sufficient to measure the intended learning target or to support the kind of judgment intended to be made.

Rubric for Tasks (Continued)

CRITERION 3: DISTORTION DUE TO BIAS
What Can Interfere with Accuracy?

Strong	Medium	Weak
1. The instructions are clear and unambiguous.	1. The instructions may leave room for erroneous interpretation of what is expected.	1. The instructions are confusing and frustrating to students.
2. The task is narrow enough in scope to be completed successfully in the time allotted. It is clear that enough time has been allotted for successful completion of the task.	2. Some students will have difficulty completing the task to the best of their ability in the time allotted. The timeline will have to be extended or the task narrowed somewhat in scope.	2. Insufficient time has been allotted for students to complete the task to the best of their ability. Either the timeline or the task, or both, will have to be reworked considerably.
3. If the task allows students to choose different tasks, it is clear that all choices will provide evidence of achievement on the same learning targets. All choices ask for the same performance or product, with approximately the same level of difficulty, and under the same conditions.	3. If the task allows students to choose different tasks, some of the choices may relate to different learning targets, or there is some variation in performance or product called for, level of difficulty, or conditions.	3. If the task allows students to choose different tasks, none of the choices relate to the same learning target, or there is considerable variation in performance or product called for, level of difficulty, and/or conditions.
4. All resources required to complete the task successfully are available to all students.	4. Some students may have difficulty obtaining the necessary resources to complete the task successfully, or one or more of the resources required will be difficult for most students to obtain.	4. Many or most students will have difficulty accessing the resources necessary to complete the task successfully.
5. Successful completion of the task does not depend on skills unrelated to the target being measured (e.g., intensive reading in a mathematics task).	5. Successful completion of the task may be slightly influenced by skills unrelated to the target being measured.	5. Successful completion of the task depends on skills unrelated to the target being measured (e.g., intensive reading in a mathematics task).
6. The task is culturally robust. Successful completion is not dependent on having had one particular cultural or linguistic background.	6. Successful completion of the task may be slightly influenced by having had one particular cultural or linguistic background.	6. The task is not culturally robust. Successful completion depends on having had one particular cultural or linguistic background.

appendix

CD Table of Contents

1. Rubric for Rubrics
2. Rubric Sampler (a collection of the 11 rubrics in Appendix C, as well as 15 others)
3. Evaluations of Selected *Rubric Sampler* and In-Text Rubrics
4. Rubric for Tasks
5. Sources of Performance Assessment Tasks, Rubrics, and Samples of Student Work